STRATEGIC STOCK TRADING

**MASTER PERSONAL FINANCE
USING WALLSTREETWINDOW STOCK INVESTING
STRATEGIES WITH STOCK MARKET TECHNICAL ANALYSIS**

MICHAEL SWANSON

ISBN: 1453666710
ISBN-13: 9781453666715

CONTENTS

INTRODUCTION

My name is Mike Swanson. I started with $15,000 in the stock market and now have over a million dollars at work in my stock trading and investment accounts. By the time you read this, there is a good chance that number will be even bigger. In 2002 I won a prestigious trading championship trophy and, in the following year, co-founded a hedge fund that I ran for several years, during which it beat the benchmark market averages. In fact, in one year it was ranked in the top forty of over five thousand hedge funds tracked by hedge-fund.net in regards to performance. I have helped tens of thousands of people who subscribe to my free and premium services at my Web site, WallStreetWindow.com, and have been interviewed by the *Wall Street Journal* and quoted all over the place, including in *Barron's*, TheStreet.com, and *Businessweek*. In this book I am going to teach you the principles behind my stock market success.

Imagine what it would be like to have as much money as you could ever want. The stock market provides this type of opportunity for you. What would you do with this money? Where would you go? All you need to do is picture one thing in your mind that you want to do to see how exciting the stock market can be for you.

You see, every day stocks go up and down and every day somehow someone makes a profit. However, most investors do not get the results they want from the stock market. Instead they miss opportunities in the market. Or they may buy a stock only to see it go down when good news comes out for what seems to be no good reason at all. Most people find the stock market to be a very confusing and illogical animal.

As a result they experience frustration and confusion. They start to think that investing is all about luck or is a game rigged against them. But there is a method to the stock market madness. There are reasons why stocks move the way they do, and all you need to do to make money is to understand them.

The reason why individual stocks appear to move without any logic to them is because everything you may think you know about the stock market and investing is wrong. Don't feel bad. If you have followed the financial news closely over the years, then you have probably noticed that most of the experts are wrong, too, at important turning points in the financial markets. Just like everyone else, they tend to get too bullish at market tops and too bearish at market bottoms.

If you read this book, everything can change for you. Once you understand the concepts in this book, you will start to see the stock market with clarity. Then, instead of tying your stomach in knots worrying about how the stock market is going to make your investments go up and down in value, you will trade stocks with confidence.

Most people just get average or worse results in the market because they don't believe in themselves. As a result, they just let their broker, who often knows less than they do, handle their money, or they just park their money in a bunch of mutual funds and let things ride at the mercy of the market. They don't learn how to invest wisely for themselves.

You see, contrary to what Wall Street experts may tell you, there is no guarantee that the stock market will just go up forever. Blind buy-and-hold investing works in secular bull markets, but does not work in a market going sideways or in a bear market. You have to be flexible and use your brain to make money in stocks. It takes work.

To be successful in stocks means taking control of your money and separating yourself from the crowd. You see, once you read this book and learn how stocks move and how to manage your money so that you cut your losing stocks early and hold on to your winning stocks, then you'll become one of the top 10 percent of the people in the stock market who make almost all of the money. You'll never be able to buy a stock or make a trade and be completely certain that it is going to go up. But if you understand the market and apply solid investing principles to put the odds in your favor, you will come to feel that making money through stock trading is indeed a sure thing.

In the end, the stock market is not a get-rich-quick mechanism. One single trade doesn't matter. Smart investing and money management do. This is what strategic stock trading is all about. The stock market is a machine that, once you understand how it ticks and apply the right principles to it, can build you wealth overtime. That said, there is nothing as exciting as getting into a hot stock and watching it blast off like a rocket.

CHAPTER 1:
ONE STOCK CAN CHANGE YOUR LIFE

In 1998 my father passed away, and I inherited $15,000 from him in a life insurance policy. At the time I was just a broke graduate student, but I always had an interest in the financial markets. So I decided to take that money and see what I could do in the stock market.

I didn't know anything about investing, so I first read about fifty books on the subject over the space of two months. I just devoured them. Some of the books were great, some not so good, but as I read more of them, I thought I had a good idea of how to invest. I could see in my mind different strategies that could work.

I took my $15,000 and put it into three stocks. The first stock was a local textile company that a friend worked at and that was on the verge of bankruptcy. He told me that he was hearing rumors that the company might get bought out, so I threw all of the ideas I got from these books to the side and decided to make a gamble.

I didn't hold this stock long, because it took it about a week for it to start to drop. I had read over and over again that you don't want to hold on to stocks that are dropping, so I quickly sold it. That much I learned. And indeed the company eventually went bankrupt and the stock went to zero. Luckily I didn't lose much. So much for hot tips and buying on rumors, I thought.

The second stock I bought was an oil rig company called Atwood Oceanics that, according to some fundamental analysis ideas I had learned, was trading at an incredibly low valuation. I made a few points on it and sold it within a week of buying it for a small gain, because of the third stock I put my money in.

I decided that this stock was so good that I had to put all of my money in it. Now I don't recommend that you ever do anything like that, and I never would now. But at the time I was just twenty-four years old and it was a small account, so I could take a big chance like that.

The Internet stocks were rising into a bubble at the time. It is hard to believe it now, but there were stocks that would go from $10 to $100 in a day. Internet companies were going public on the stock market with initial public offerings (IPOs) and seeing their stocks open up at crazy valuations and prices.

One day while in a Barnes & Noble looking at investment books, I angled over to the magazine section and bought a copy of *Businessweek*. I ran to my apartment and started to go through it. On the back page, I saw an article about an

Internet company called CBS Marketwatch and how it was about to go public. The writer expected it to be a huge IPO, projecting the stock to possibly open up over $100 a share.

He also mentioned that its biggest shareholder was a parent technology company called Data Broadcasting. The article talked about how when other companies of the past few months had spun off parts of themselves and taken them public, they had seen their stock prices rocket up before these IPOs started trading. Many of these parent stocks doubled in value into the day the IPO of their spin-off company started to trade. Some even tripled. I could see how the same thing could happen again with Data Broadcasting.

Now this doesn't happen anymore, so don't try it. This was back during the Internet stock bubble days of 1999, the greatest year for the Nasdaq composite ever. At the time, though, I could just see how this stock could turn my little account into a big account. I could look in the future and feel how exciting this could be. In less than two weeks, the big CBS Marketwatch IPO would happen, and I expected Data Broadcasting to go up as the day got closer.

So I put all of my money into this one stock at around $18 a share. Every day I would come home and log on to my computer and head over to Yahoo! Finance to read the Data Broadcasting message board. On there I found people just like me who believed in the stock. People who knew DBCC would go to the moon and make all of us rich.

There were a few people who doubted it, but for every one person that dared to doubt, there were twenty who shouted them down. Owning the stock was exciting. Not only could I imagine getting rich, but communicating with the people on the message board made me feel like I was part of something big. One man on the board said that he believed in the stock so much that he decided to take a loan out on his house in order to put everything he owned and more into the stock. He said it would make him a millionaire.

I came up with a simple plan. I looked back at all of the other recent spinoff IPOs that occurred and found that when the parent company's stock rose into the IPO, once the IPO started to trade it crashed back down to where it started from. That meant DBCC would probably go up to $36, $40, or even $50 by the time of the IPO but would be back down to below $18 weeks after it came out.

So I planned to simply sell for a big profit when the IPO hit. A simple plan, and it seemed to work. My shares slowly went up. They went to $20 and then back down to $18, which made me a little uneasy, but everyone on the board said to just hold on. And they were right, because the next thing I knew the stock went through $20 and up to $23. Then to $25. Within days the IPO would start to trade and I'd have my payday.

I told the people on the board about my plan to sell out. Some of them said this was a mistake. They said this was a long-term investment and would go up even more as CBS Marketwatch grew. When I pointed out that all of the parent companies went up and then dropped with their IPO spinoffs, they just said that this time would be different.

I didn't believe them. On IPO day, DBCC went over $40 a share. I don't remember the exact price I sold out at, but I more than doubled my money. Within two weeks the stock fell below where I bought it at. I don't know what happened to the guy that took a loan out on his house. I don't know if he sold his shares or just held on, but on days like today when I think about this story, I wonder.

I know this, though. That stock changed my life. Watching it go up and then selling it for a huge gain was one of the most exciting things I had done until then. I got a little too excited, in fact. For someone who once worked at Walmart, I had never had that much money before nor made money that easily. I thought I would never have to work again.

I was wrong. With some more trades I managed to turn my $15,000 into over $50,000 in just a few weeks, but within ten months I turned that $50,000 into $7,000. I almost lost everything. I chased stocks recommended by analysts on TV, written about in magazines, and talked about on the Internet, only to watch them drop after I bought them. If there were hot rumors, I had to get involved, because I didn't want to miss out.

I got to a point where I had to face reality. Either I had to start to make money in the stock market or I would lose everything and get taken out of the game. That meant realizing that I had not been investing or trading with any sort of strategy at all. All I had been doing is throwing my money at the market and gambling.

But I knew from those books and studies that I had done that you could use a strategy to make money in the market. I just hadn't been doing it. So I sat down and decided on a strategy that I would stick with that was best suited for the current market environment.

Within a few weeks, I doubled my money again. After twelve more months, I turned my $7,000 into over $100,000 and have never looked back since.

The point of this is simple. Most people do not invest in the stock market with any sort of game plan at all. They buy stocks on hot news and tips and have no idea what to do after they buy them. They don't know how to tell if a stock is really going to go up or if the people spreading the news and rumors are just trying to get them to buy so they can sell their shares to them.

To make money in the stock market, you have to have a strategic game plan and stick with it. My first year in the stock market taught me that, because I got myself in a situation where I either had to do it or lose everything. By the time you are done with this book, I hope you will be able to incorporate the ideas in it to make a game plan of your own. The first thing you need to do is realize that you can't chase rumors and news like a turkey with its head cut off; instead, bet on real, sustainable trends that can make you money. The few who do that in the stock market are the few that make all of the money.

CHAPTER 2:
INVEST ALONGSIDE THE SMART MONEY

Have you ever bought a stock that had great news only to see it drop afterwards? Maybe the stock just came out with a positive press release. You saw the stock rise and bought it, thinking that the great news surely meant that stock would keep going higher, only to feel the pain of losing money when it didn't. It doesn't seem right. Stocks should always go up on good news and not fall some of the time when good news is announced, but they don't. Sometimes they drop instead.

Or maybe you bought a stock in a company that you just know is good, only to lose money anyway. Maybe it was a company that you know is growing fast. Or a company that analysts upgraded and are projecting great earnings growth for in the future. But the stock dropped anyway. It makes no sense. It doesn't seem fair, because it seems like you should always be rewarded for believing in and investing in good companies.

But stocks are not companies. They are pieces of paper that people value based on what they think is going to happen in the future. Sometimes stocks do go up when the news is good, as it seems they should, but many times they don't. This fact makes the stock market appear to be totally confusing to people, because it doesn't make much sense to them. How can stocks fall when it seems like they should go up?

The reason why stocks don't always go up on good news is because stocks and the stock market as a whole tend to discount news. Smart money buys ahead of good news in anticipation of the news and sells before bad news come out. As a result there is a tendency for stocks to actually go up before good news comes out and often drop afterwards, especially if the news has been widely anticipated. This is what happened after I sold Data Broadcasting, for example.

This sort of thing happens all of the time. If you owned shares in a company and had reason to believe that it was going to go bankrupt would you wait until its stock went to zero before selling, or would you sell right now and get what you have left out of it first? The same logic holds for positive developments. Smart money doesn't wait for good news to buy, but buys ahead of the news.

That's why a stock will often top out right when the good news comes out. Smart money traders have already factored the news into the stock price by buying and moving it up before the news is released and becomes public knowledge. So they take their profits and sell to the masses that tend to just buy into the hype.

This is why it's impossible for you to make money in the stock market by just chasing news. And why it's difficult to make money on analyst recommendations, too. It's not that the analysts are crooks and trying to trick you, but that smarter people than the analysts already figured out the story, so when the analysts upgrade a stock, all of the good things they are projecting are often already priced in.

This puts the average investor always one step behind the market when he or she chases news. But it doesn't have to be like that for you. You must realize that most events are preceded by many smaller events and multiple warning signs of what is to come. It is on these things that intelligent investment decisions must be made. Stock prices move in anticipation of big events that catch the attention of the masses. And, of course, the crowd often over discounts a news event. This is how stocks can get to extremely high and low valuations and provide opportunities that you can use to truly buy low and sell high at the right times.

This is why at key market turning points the crowd is always wrong. Making money in the stock market is all about being positioned ahead of the crowd. What I want you to take from this is the following: Do not obsess over the day-to-day activity in the stock market and the news. Do not buy stocks simply because news is good or sell just because the news might be bad, either.

Most people that buy on news instinctively know this, but just get caught up in the excitement of the moment. As a result, everyone searches for an inside edge. That is why people get attracted to stock stories where someone tells you about some future development happening in a company that is going to make the stock price go up.

You could get the tip from someone you know working at the company or read about in a magazine or a newsletter. But the problem is, most of the time these tips don't work out either, because they aren't really secret knowledge at all. There is no way you can know more about a company secondhand than the corporate executives and their friends, their competitors, and the few analysts who are true experts on the company and its industry do. These people make up the smart money that creates sustainable moves in a stock. When you buy on a secondhand tip that you hear or read about, you are trying to outsmart these people.

That's a game you really cannot win. But you actually do have an edge that you probably don't even realize. You do not have to outsmart these people at all. The people you need to outsmart are the masses of other people who buy on stock tips, react to market news, and invest with little knowledge of what is going on. Think of this as the dumb money.

To invest better than the masses, all you need to do is to start to look at the stock market itself and understand the price action of the market and individual stocks. Then you will start to identify trends that you can make money from.

You have to realize that the stock market tends to move in trends that really are not changed by what news happens to come out in any given single day or even what the market does in one day. These trends last for weeks, months, and sometimes years and move in cycles. It is by identifying these trends that one makes money in the stock market on a consistent basis, year in and year out.

To say that the stock market moves in trends means that stock prices move in a pattern. Like the laws of physics, these trends continue until they come to an end. So to make money in the stock market, all you need to do is identify what the current trend is and invest accordingly until that trend changes. To do that, you first need to become a student of stock price movements.

The fancy term for this in investmentspeak is technical analysis—making investment decisions based on the price and volume action of a stock or the market as a whole. The idea behind it is that all of the known information is already known by the people who are influencing the price of a stock. This includes current earnings and knowledge about future earnings, products, and changes inside of the company and the economic sector that it is a part of. Even inside information is factored into a stock price. There is no way you can know all of this information yourself. But you don't need to. All you need to do is understand how stock prices move and you'll find yourself at times investing when insiders are, without even trying to.

CHAPTER 3:
LEARN TO READ STOCK PRICE MOVEMENTS

When I first got into trading, Internet stocks were the biggest movers in the stock market. Data Broadcasting gave me just a little taste of what was happening. So many stocks were going so high at the time that many of them became totally dissociated from their underlying companies.

You can figure out what the stock market is valuing a company at by taking the number of stock shares outstanding for it and multiplying it by the price of the shares. This will give you the market capitalization figure for a stock. There were Internet stocks with market caps over a billion dollars that were losing money. Priceline.com, for example, was losing tens of millions of dollars a year and was being priced as if it were worth more than the five biggest airlines combined.

From a valuation standpoint it made no sense, but these were the stocks that were going up the most and making people rich. And I wanted to be a part of that, even though I knew that one day, many of these stocks would end up going to zero, because eventually many of their underlying companies would end up bankrupt. So I needed a strategy I could use to buy and sell them. It was when I came up with one and stuck with it that I started to make money.

What was driving these stocks was pure investor psychology, which can be completely irrational at times. Studying earnings, valuation, or news stories was useless in knowing what to do with these stocks. If you got in a good one that went up a lot, you would have to sell it to make money, because it would eventually collapse. This was not a game of investing in something forever, but of getting in and then getting out when the getting was good. That meant selling to a greater fool and making sure you wouldn't be the last one out the door.

I had to figure a way to do that, and the only thing I had to go by was studying the movement of the stock prices themselves to try to identify some repeating patterns that I could take advantage of. And that's what I did.

There have been many times over the years that I have made such exact forecasts of stock prices that people think I have some sort of super intuitive powers when it comes to the market. That really isn't true. I simply learned some simple stock patterns early on and can now see them at a glance when I look at the market or an individual stock.

Stocks simply trade in trends. They are either moving higher in an uptrend, falling in a downtrend, or moving in a sideways trend, and those trends continue until they are over.

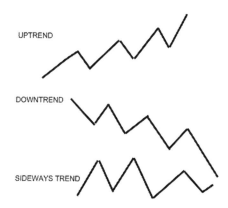

If you take a simple line chart of a stock, you'll see that it goes through uptrends and downtrends. On a line chart, the lines are either going up or down. They form peaks and valleys.

Take a look at a sixty-minute line chart. There is a very simple pattern you'll see. When a stock is in a downtrend it will continue to make lower lows, meaning each valley will be lower than the last one, and each peak is lower than the last one, too. Prices are going down. The lines keep going lower from left to right across a chart.

Then, in an uptrend, a stock will make higher highs and higher lows. Each peak is higher than the last one, and each valley ends up forming at a point higher than the last one too. The prices keep going up. The lines move from left to right across the chart in an upward manner. This is a simple uptrend.

But there are often transition periods between uptrends and downtrends on a line chart in which a stock that has been in a downtrend will stop making lower lows. All of a sudden a new low will form higher than the last one. This could just be a short-lived fake-out move, but if the stock manages to go through its last peak, than it will make a higher high to break the downtrend pattern.

If it then begins to make higher highs and higher lows, it will be in an uptrend. What you will have seen is a stock that has ended a downtrend and begun a new uptrend. The change just took place right in front of your eyes, and it is by recognizing such changes that trading decisions are made.

This is the basic definition of an uptrend and downtrend in a stock. It is the very first simple pattern that I learned myself when it came to the stock market and still apply to it whenever I look at it. Just looking at this pattern evolve and change at times, and taking note of it when it does, is what makes some people think I have an intuitive feel for the market.

But in order to know the pattern this well, you have to do more than just read about it or see it once. You need to spend several weeks watching it play out on a few of your favorite stocks and a couple of the market indices. Do this. Yes, you can go back and look at some stock charts and see how this pattern played out in the past. You should do that, and you can do it using charts plotted out in hourly, daily, and weekly time frames.

But to really grasp it and get a true feel for it, you also are going to have to watch it play out over time. Doing this will cause you to think about what you are seeing on a deeper level and to anticipate what happens when you see patterns start to change on the charts.

Then you'll start to learn. You'll start to focus on what stocks and the market are really doing instead of just the news and stories around them. Then you'll come to get a feel for price action.

What causes these price trends is the fact that there are different sources of buying and selling pressure that come into the market and with different motivations—from short-term day traders to the real smart money that bases its decisions not on current news, but on real knowledge of events likely to come in the future. Those are the people who really move the stock market, and although it is about impossible for you to have the knowledge that they have, you can identify when they are accumulating stocks so that you can buy along with them.

When you go beyond the insiders, there are basically three types of people that buy stocks. There are the masses of people that just impulsively buy stocks without any game plan at all simply because other people are doing so. They hear hot tips from these people or stories about why the stock is going to go up. Or they may buy simply due to a news story they hear about on TV. They buy at a top and then, when a stock drops so much that they can't take it anymore, they sell near a bottom and lose money.

Then there are people who buy momentum, because they expect that the economic conditions behind a price rise or the price action itself makes them believe that higher prices are to come. Such a trader does not try to buy on a bottom or expect to be able to. In fact, he prefers and is perfectly willing at times to buy when a stock makes a new high if he expects it will go up even higher. He buys and holds until he thinks that conditions are turning bearish or that the price advance has gone so far that it has made his stock overvalued. He then sells out. These traders often cause the best stocks to rise rapidly when they break out to new highs.

Lastly, there is the conservative type that likes to buy on dips and can hardly be talked into buying when a stock makes a new high. He reasons that prices often go through temporary corrections within strong upward trends, and the best way to get in is to use them to their advantage. He may say to himself at times, "It seems stocks should advance from these prices, but I can't predict things exactly, and prices have often declined a bit when I feel just as bullish as I do now. So I will place orders to buy on a drop. These buy-high momentum traders are crazy, and there is no knowing what passing breeze might make them sell and cause a temporary pullback."

Such men have neither the time nor disposition to watch stocks trade tick by tick and nearly always disclaim any ability to predict short-term price movements, but are ready to take advantage of small downward fluctuations when they occur. They often have plenty of capital, so they can easily accomplish this buying on a large scale. These type of traders and investors create support levels in stocks during bull markets.

What you need to realize is that what really moves stocks are buyers and sellers and their psychological motivations. If you plot out a stock on a chart, you'll see that stock prices form areas of support and resistance where multiple peaks and valleys keep occurring at the same price points. If a stock falls to a certain area and then bottoms there over and over again, that is considered to be an area of support, while resistance is a price level where a stock repeatedly has peaked out at.

Support levels are formed by conservative types who buy on pullbacks. That support will continue to exist until the conservative types have bought all of the stock that they can or want to. Then their buying disappears, and if a stock falls back to support again, it will go through that support level and make another leg down.

Resistance is formed by people who repeatedly sell when a stock rises to a certain level, thereby preventing the stock from going higher. Just as support disappears when the dip buyers run out of money, resistance levels fade away when all of the people who keep selling at a certain price level run out of stock to sell. Then the stock clears resistance and begins a new upward move.

Now I've suggested that you take a look at short-term sixty-minute trends to get a feel for these price movements. In the end, though, these same type of patterns play out on daily and weekly charts where more long-lasting and profitable trends occur. While the shorter-term trends often are influenced by fickle investor psychology and temporary news items, the longer-term trends are linked to real fundamentals and the state of the economy. That is where the big money is made.

CHAPTER 4:
WHAT REALLY MAKES A STOCK GO UP

Over the years I have made lots of money in individual stocks and have a large following, thanks to my successful stock recommendations. However, one reason for this is that I only recommend good stocks when I see them. Most people subscribe to stock market advisory services with the intention of hitting it big by just buying someone else's stock picks, but the problem is there are times in the market when it is best not to buy stocks at all, and only a few times a year when huge opportunities line up.

In fact, in any given year, there is normally a decent-sized correction that enables you to buy stocks at huge bargain prices. Unfortunately the average person is unable to wait for such moments, and almost all advisory services cater to the masses by giving them stock picks on a constant basis with no regard to what is going on in the stock market. The tough truth is that most people simply crave the gambling action they can get out of the stock market and don't have the right mentality to truly build wealth over time. Some want to listen only to hype.

In the fall of 2007, I told my readers that I believed we were just beginning a brutal bear market. I eventually told them that I would no longer give them any more stock recommendations until the bear market ended, because I thought that they should be as defensive as possible in the stock market and look to make money by actually betting against the major market averages. I even told them in the summer of 2008 that I was gravely concerned that the stock market could completely collapse and I begged people to get out of it.

A lot of people got extremely angry when I made these calls, and I undoubtedly lost some readers because of it. But it was the right thing to do, because the stock market crashed in the worst bear market seen since the Great Depression. Then, in the summer of 2009, I started to recommend stocks again, and my readers and I were able to make some handsome profits in many of them. Several of them went up over 100% in just a few months.

The point of this isn't to brag to you, but to tell you that you cannot simply throw money at individual stocks at just any given moment and expect to make money. The stock market simply doesn't work that way, and there are times when it is best not to even fool with buying individual stocks. I have no interest in buying stocks for entertainment or making recommendations just because the typical beginner craves them all of the time. The stock market truly rewards diligence and patience and punishes the mad gambler and the lazy.

To really make money in stocks, you have to know when to buy them and fully understand what makes stocks go up. I've talked with you a little bit about price action and will go into much greater detail about it in a bit, but first you must understand the fundamental economic factors that really move stocks.

Stocks do not trade in a vacuum. They are influenced by the broad trend of the stock market and the prospects of the economic sector that they are in. Stocks tend to move together in groups all commonly influenced by the economic niche they are in. In fact, sectors and the broad trend of the stock market influences stock prices more than the characteristics of an individual stock do.

For instance, individual car companies tend to rise and fall together, and so do retailers, oil companies, computer companies, and anything else you can think of, because they all share many of the same business prospects, opportunities, and challenges. It is simple logic. If you own a business in your town and the town experiences an influx in population, then you can expect to see your sales grow along with your competitors'. However, if unemployment goes up or people start to leave, then you can expect your sales to flatten or shrink along with everyone else's. The business trends for sectors do not change quickly. Trends can last for years and they rarely change overnight. That is why you get long sideways phases after a major bottom in a stock.

What makes a stock good to own, though, is its presence in a niche in the economy going from a recessionary trough to a new, expansive upswing, or coming out of nowhere and being a source of new innovation that will translate into earnings growth. Since other companies in the niche are in a similar position, they all tend to rise and eventually fall together.

That makes watching stock sectors a key to investing. Luckily, there are different stock market advisory services and software programs that break the stock market up into sectors and place individual stocks into sectors so you can see what is going on. For instance, I use TC2000, made by Worden Brothers, Inc., which allows me to look at the U.S. stock market as over 250 individual sectors. I look at these sectors to discover which ones are at optimal entry points and then look at the leading stocks and companies in those sectors for buy candidates.

The economy goes through periods of contraction and expansion known as the business cycle. Since the stock market discounts future news and is forward looking, it tends to go up during an expansionary phase and top out before the economy does. It then will often go through a bear market in which the stock market goes lower and lower and finally bottoms out before the recessionary trough is formed. That is why, when new bull markets begin, usually the news remains negative until the bull market is well under way and why news can seem great at the beginning of a bear market, too.

The best time to buy a stock is after it has already gone through a bear market and then made a major bottom and is just beginning a new bull run. This is how you make huge money. This is how you get in positions that will go up twofold and often more. That means buying at the point at which the maximum return can be made with very little risk.

I'm not talking about buying on an exact bottom, though. It is very difficult—impossible really—for you to buy a stock on the exact bottom after an extended decline. If you happen to do it, then you got lucky, and you really don't need to in order to make big money anyway, because after a major bottom, stocks tend to just go sideways for several months before they go into a new bull phase. It is during this sideways phase that insiders build their positions.

It often takes months for a stock to bottom and then make the transition into a new bull run, and the transition phase usually simply consists of a lot of back and forth movement in which, to the untrained observer, nothing seems to be happening. In fact, during the transition phase, most of the news around a stock is bad and scares people away.

Insiders tend to accumulate huge positions in a stock and have a long-term holding period. Yes, they may sell when they see cloud storms up ahead, but they tend to build heavy positions after a stock has gone through a bear market of its own and they see signs of better economic prospects ahead. It is at these times that it is best to take a position in a stock. Of course, no insider is going to tell you when he is buying so you can buy with him, but what you can do is be able to recognize these great buy points in a stock so that you can end up buying when the insider does anyway.

That means understanding how economic sectors move in relationship to one another and how to spot the great buy points in individual stocks.

CHAPTER 5:
RIDING A STOCK SECTOR FROM TROUGH TO PEAK

Most people buy stocks simply because they are down. They see a stock that has gone up a lot over time that all of a sudden drops. I advocate buying stocks at times on just such corrections, but you have to know what you are doing to be able to determine whether what you are seeing is really a buying opportunity or the start of a big new downtrend or, heaven forbid, a bear market.

Most people do not know how to tell the difference, and I hate those times that a bear market strikes even though I tend to make money in them myself. The problem is, I really care about my readers and want them to succeed in the stock market, but in bear markets the masses of people will not listen to those that tell them to protect themselves, because they get caught up in hype and premature bottom guessing. Only people who have paid attention to me for a long time and have experienced my track record for themselves really listen to what I say at such moments.

You simply cannot buy just because things are dropping. Trying to catch a falling knife is the most dangerous thing that an amateur investor can try to do. In the fall of 2000, I warned people week after week that we were just starting a horrible bear market. I received feedback from many people who listened and saved themselves, but also got e-mails from people who didn't or who got caught up in a bad situation.

One woman e-mailed me and told me that she had taken out a $30,000 cash advance on a credit card and put the money in her brokerage account, where she bought some high-flying tech stocks that she heard about on TV. They got cut in half, and in response she took out another big loan and doubled down on them. Now they had fallen more and she e-mailed me asking me what she should do.

It was a horrible story and I felt very bad for her. There wasn't much I could say or do to help. But I want you to promise never to do anything like that. Never overextend yourself in the stock market, and don't double down on losers.

I also got e-mails from other people who weren't getting wiped out like that, but were still losing money because they were trying to buy falling stocks in a vicious bear market. In 2008 I warned people that we were in a bear market and got feedback from many people who didn't listen to my advice and tried to buy into falling stocks only to lose tons of money. I hated that this happened to them.

The vast majority of investors try to do this in bear markets and lose money. Don't do this. Do not buy stocks simply because they are down. Yes, the best time to buy stocks is when they are low, but you do not have to buy on an exact bottom to get in at a cheap price. In fact, most of the time after a stock bottoms, it spends months afterwards doing nothing but going sideways. It isn't until the end of this sideways stabilization pattern that they really go up, so buying on exact bottoms doesn't really make you any extra money anyway, and trying to guess such bottoms is incredibly risky unless you know what you are doing and are disciplined enough to cut losses in case you guessed too soon.

It takes time for a bear market to end and turn into a bull market. Big trends in the stock market do not change overnight. Some sectors lead the economy while others lag, and there are times when developments particular to an individual sector cause it to seem to trade in its own world separate to what is going on everywhere else. In each bull market, too, there are often new sectors that lead the new bull market that didn't in the last one, because there are always new areas of innovation and growth in the economy.

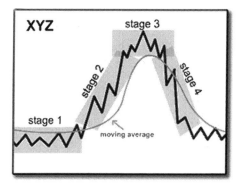

Markets, sectors, and stocks all tend to have a distinctive cyclical pattern to them—I like to say they go through stages. Stage one is a sideways consolidation period following a bear market. Stage two is a bull market, stage three a topping phase, and stage four a bear market. We'll just focus on sectors for now.

During a stage three bull market top, almost all of the news focusing on a sector is incredibly positive. Analysts are projecting huge earnings growth for the future, while the stocks often hold big valuations as a result of these expectations. However, often insiders are selling out at this time, because they believe that they have seen a peak in growth for their industry or else a recession is looming in the future. A top comes and eventually, as the future the insiders see up ahead becomes a reality, the stocks can often crash, because the big valuations have set them up for huge selling when investors get caught off guard.

A classic example came with the home builder Toll Brothers when its CEO sold hundreds of millions worth of stock at the end of the real estate boom in 2007 and 2008 while the stock—and the home-building sector—remained a favorite of most Wall Street analysts. A year later it became clear to everyone that the real estate market had made a major top in the United States around the time this CEO was cashing out, and the stocks got hammered for massive losses as a result.

After a major top, a sector will go into a bear market stage four decline, but during this decline more often than not the analysts still stay positive for much of the time, thinking that any slowdown in the economy or earnings is just a temporary blip and that all pullbacks are buying opportunities.

The public, which got conditioned by the last bull market to buy dips, jumps in, thinking all down days are buying days, but insiders and the smart money players know better and feed shares to them. Some even profit by betting against stocks via short-selling. This goes on until finally the smart money sees that the price has fallen so much that it makes no sense to sell anymore. The smart money stops selling and finally a bottom comes in the sector.

What you need to realize is that a bottom doesn't come when all of a sudden the smart money starts to buy and thereby makes everything go up, but when it stops selling. Bear markets end when the selling pressure comes to an end, and more often than not this process comes with a panic washout on the part of the public and so-called professional traders on Wall Street who really are not much better at investing than the average man in the street. The mediocre performance of most mutual funds proves this to be a fact.

Now you can quickly identify what stage a sector, market, or stock is in by looking at its price in relation to its 200-day moving average—which is an indicator created by looking at the average price over 200 days. If the price is above this moving average and the moving average is sloped upwards, then you are looking at a stage two bull market. However, if the price is below this moving average and that moving average is trending down, then you are looking at a stage four bear market. You can find this indicator and use it with your favorite stock on several free stock charting sites available on the Internet. One I use often is stockcharts.com.

The above chart is a chart of the S&P 500 from stockcharts.com. The moving average in the chart is the 200-day moving average. From 2003 till late 2007, the S&P 500 was in a stage two bull market, because this moving average was sloping up and the price of the S&P 500 stayed above this moving average. Then the S&P 500 entered a bear market by going below this moving average and staying below it as the moving average turned down.

It is during a stage one consolidation phase following a bear market that the insiders and smart money build a position, and that you need to be most alert. The ironic thing, though, is that during this time, the general public has no interest at all in the sector. The news generally is bad, earnings growth often has been negative the past few quarters, and the financial media, which talk more about stocks going up and hot news items, report very little on the sector. However, despite all of the negativity over the sector, the stocks that make it up simply are going sideways in a stage one basing phase.

What is happening is that the smart money has put a floor on the sector by accumulating shares, because either the valuations for the sector have become so cheap that it is ridiculous to sell or else they see light at the end of a recessionary tunnel. The sector is not going up yet, though. It's just going sideways in a range, and that fact either bores most people or frustrates them into thinking that nothing is good about the sector anymore. So the dumb money keeps selling as the smart money accumulates.

Just as the smart money helps put a floor on prices, the dumb money keeps a lid on them, selling on up moves in the sector and thinking that they have to be temporary because the news is still bad. This can go on for weeks, months, and sometimes even up to a year. During this time the 200-day moving average flattens out and prices fluctuate above and below it.

As the end of the stage one consolidation phase nears, the buying pressure from the smart money begins to pick up. In the individual stocks that make up the sector, volume often increases, too. The trading range begins to narrow as the peaks and lows of the sector form closer together. Then the dumb money simply runs out of shares to sell. Buyers take over and a big upside breakout through the consolidation phase takes place, and a new stage two bull phase begins.

The optimal buy point occurs right towards the end of this consolidation phase, just before a new bull market begins. It is at this point that you can buy a stock, watch it quickly rise twofold and then go even higher from there, and get in with very limited risk. It is where fortunes are made.

Often, though, as the new bull market begins, the news can still be negative, and there is usually a lot of doubt among people about whether the move is for real or not. The masses remember the pain they experienced getting excited over the false rallies that came with the last bear market and worry that this rally is probably a false one, too. So they don't buy at the start of the bull move, but wait until much later when the news gets better and the Wall Street analysts and talking heads on television tell them they need to buy. And then eventually the cycle repeats itself once another top is formed.

The stage one basing phase for the energy sector from July 2002 till April 2003 is circled below.

After a bear market bottom it is common to see dozens of sectors go through such basing phases that last for months and precede a new bull market.

CHAPTER 6:
HOW TO BUY TOMORROW'S BIG WINNERS TODAY

I never read magazines for investment ideas anymore and pay no attention to what the Wall Street analysts recommend. I learned that buying a hot stock tip and losing money just isn't very exciting.

What is exciting is finding a sector that is just about to start a new bull market, buying the best stocks in it, and then watching those stocks go up faster than anything else in the stock market. It's just that no one on TV hands you such a wonderful gift. If they did, everyone would strike it rich in the stock market. Instead you have to know where to look to find such opportunities for yourself, and once you do it's an incredible thing.

Warren Buffett talks about a simple way that an investor can improve their returns. Imagine having a punch card with twenty slots on it. Each time you make a new investment, you punch one of the slots. You only get to make twenty investment decisions over your lifetime. What would you do?

One thing I bet you wouldn't do is go by some random stock tip. One point Buffett makes with his punch card is that you are presented with a constant stream of opportunities. Every day the stock market does something, and at any given moment someone is telling you to invest in this or that. Thinking about a mental punch card makes you slow down and make sure you make the best decisions that you can.

The second bit of wisdom you need to get from this is that you do not need to make a lot of successful investment decisions to create remarkable results. Just a few smart decisions can create life-changing returns for you. For example, Buffett bought the *Washington Post* for just over $10 million. Today it is worth over a billion dollars.

Talk about a return! The trick to big-time investing is to find an investment that justifies taking a shot at the mental punch card. I have found that the best way to do this is to align yourself with the smart money and buy into a sector just starting a new bull market.

For instance, in the winter of 2002 I started to buy gold stocks. Gold and gold stocks had been in a bear market for five years and a secular bear market for over twenty years up until then. The price of gold fell to $250 an ounce. Gold and gold stocks were poised to break out of a stage one base when I first recommended them.

Insider trading data showed that corporate CEOs and insiders of gold companies were accumulating shares like crazy. Within two years the XAU gold stock index doubled off of its bear market low while leading gold stocks went up three times that rate. There were gold stocks that I bought for less than $1 that ultimately went up over $10 a share. Today gold is well over $1,000 an ounce and looks to go much higher in the years to come.

Every year there is a similar big opportunity somewhere in a stock sector in the United States or in a global market elsewhere. The best way to find these great buys is to watch what sectors are holding up when the market has a decline or pullback. When a sector holds up while the rest of the stock market drops, it means that money is flowing into that sector and keeping it from declining while everything else around it is falling. There are still a lot of sell orders hitting these strong sectors, but the smart money is using them to increase their position. It takes a lot of buying pressure to keep a stock or a sector from dropping during a stock market correction, and normally, once a market decline comes to an end, the sectors that hold up the most during the decline lead the next rally.

Gauging the relative strength of one sector against another or in comparison with a broad market index, such as the DOW or S&P 500, is easy to do. All you have to do is divide the price performance of one thing against what you want to compare it with to see which one is performing the strongest.

For example, in the first few months of 2009, the U.S. markets experienced a sharp correction along with most global markets that caused a 27% drop in the S&P 500. During this correction, the Chinese stock market did not fall as much as the S&P 500. If you had divided the price of the FXI China ETF and the S&P 500, you would have created a relative strength ratio on a stock chart. FXI had greater relative strength in comparison with the S&P 500, because this ratio was rising.

Once the March 2009 correction came to an end, a rally occurred in almost all markets across the globe. The S&P 500 rallied 43% from its March low to its June high, but FXI rallied 79% in the same time frame. The strong relative strength that preceded this rally tipped anyone looking off to the fact that smart money was flowing into China—thereby causing stocks in China to hold up in comparison with the rest of the world. It was no surprise, then, that China stocks rallied more than U.S. stocks once the market bottomed.

This same type of analysis works when you compare individual sectors to the broad market averages too. Using TC2000 stock software, I can quickly run relative strength comparison of the sectors with each other and the broad market averages. I also do similar analyses of different world market indices. This way I can identify where the smart money is flowing in the United States and in the entire world.

As a general rule of thumb, you want to invest in the strongest sectors of the market and look for those sectors and entry points in them during market pullbacks and corrections. When it comes to individual stocks, you want to invest in the ones that lead their sectors. In every sector there are companies that provide it leadership through innovation and earnings growth. The stocks of these companies tend to perform the best when the sector is in an upswing and drop the least when it is in a correction.

That means relative strength analysis is important when it comes to individual stocks, too, but the way to make the best use of it is not to compare a stock's performance with that of a broad market average like the S&P 500, but with an index of the sector of which it is a component. For instance, you can compare the performance of the shares of several dozen oil companies with that of the XLE Energy sector exchange traded fund to identify the leading energy stocks.

Most of the time when someone buys a stock, they don't pay any attention at all to what the other stocks in its niche are doing, but sector analysis is more important than the characteristics of a company—whether it be its earnings or the action in the stock itself—because stocks inside a sector tend to rise and fall together no matter what the earnings and analyst predictions are. That is why relative strength and stage analysis are such powerful tools and where I always start when I analyze a stock.

So the bottom line when it comes to looking for stocks to buy is this: I first look at the sectors to identify what area of the stock market—and sometimes the world market—that I want to invest in using relative strength analysis. Then I look for sectors coming out of stage one bases that have the most upside potential. And then, finally, I look for the strongest stocks inside the sector itself to create a list of potential buy candidates among the leading companies and stocks in a sector positioned to go much higher. Only then do I examine the individual stocks themselves and the underlying fundamentals of the companies they represent in order to gauge their potential to go up. I use relative strength and technical analysis to determine what is going on and then examine things further to figure out why.

CHAPTER 7:
THE MOST PROFITABLE STOCK PATTERN YOU CAN BUY

Never get married to a stock. The investment game is about one thing, and that is making money. It isn't about feeling good just because you own a stock. There are people who are motivated to get into the stock market because they think that the elites are in the stock market, so it makes them feel important to be a part of it. When you look to buy a stock, you must understand that you are buying a piece of paper—nothing more.

Many people also get caught up in thinking that just because they own a stock, they are an owner in a company, and they fall in love with that idea. Even if a company has great management and great earnings, a stock can still go down at times if the sector it is in or the stock market as a whole is on hard times. If you think of yourself as a loyal shareholder, it doesn't seem fair to have to suffer at times like this.

But as a shareholder, often you are not even the most important stakeholder in the company. There are two types of stocks—preferred and common stocks. Then you also have bondholders, who lend money to companies. When a company goes bankrupt, bondholders and owners of preferred stock get any proceeds from liquidation first. Common stockholders almost always get completely wiped out. When you buy shares off of the stock exchange, you are almost always buying common stock, so you are not considered one of the most important shareholders in the company. You may occasionally be asked to vote on changes in management or proposals brought up ahead of shareholder meetings, but that is the extent of your rights as a common stock shareholder.

I am telling you this because I don't want you to get caught up in feeling that you are special just because you bought a stock. It doesn't make you an important person. Some people think that they should buy stocks in companies that they like, that have good news, or that are talked about a lot. That leads people into a mentality of buying and holding forever, and at some point you are going to have to sell and take profits or cut your losses if a stock goes down instead of up. If you refuse to sell when necessary, then you aren't cut out for stock investing.

What is more, stock prices do not always reflect the underlying value of the company they represent. Stock prices fluctuate day by day, and rarely do the fortunes of a company change so quickly. There are times when stock prices fall below what a company is worth, thereby providing you with an opportunity to make money by buying shares at a low price, and times when a stock price goes up so high that it no longer represents reality and you need to sell and take your profits. Stocks trade on investor expectations and psychology, which can change on a dime.

This means that when it comes to buying a stock, after I look at the state of the sector that it is a part of, I look at the trading and volume action in the stock to determine if it poised for a big move higher. I look at what buyers and sellers are doing with the stock itself and not my feelings or expectations of what a company is going to do. In the end, when you buy or own a stock, you are speculating that other people will eventually pay a higher price for the stock than you are now.

You make money in the stock market by understanding when the optimal time to buy a stock is. The good news is that there are repeatable patterns you can watch for that occur before big moves in stocks. There are so many different types of stock patterns, though, that it is best to focus on only the most profitable ones. I basically look through stocks in top sectors for these patterns and then study the company and the valuation of the stock to get an idea of how high it can go once it starts to go up.

But I look for certain patterns first, because I only want to get in stocks that are poised to jump up fast. There are two basic patterns I look for when it comes to individual stocks. First is to find a stock breaking out of a stage one base, and second is a stock that has already broken out, but is pausing before rising again. In fact, this second pattern can actually be more profitable than the first over the short term.

The stage one basing pattern is the same pattern I told you about when looking for sectors that are entering bull markets. You basically look for a stock that has been stabilizing after a stage four bear market. Its 200 and 150-day moving averages are now going sideways and the stock has bounced up and down in a channel, so you can see clear support and resistance areas in it.

Ideally you also should see trading volume in the stock pick up. For instance, if a stock has been trading 100,000 shares in average daily volume, if it starts to trade 200,000 shares a day, then often something big happens. When this occurs towards the end of a basing phase, it indicates that money is suddenly flowing into the stock, usually from smart money insiders. It won't be long before the sellers that are responsible for the resistance on the stock get taken out. Once that happens, the stock will likely enter a new stage two bull market.

Unless the stock market has been rallying like crazy the past few weeks, the stock should also be performing better than the major market averages. If the market has been weak and the stock has been holding up at the same time, then this is a huge positive indication that the smart money is accumulating the stock.

Often the volatility in the stock shrinks right before it breaks out of resistance. What this means is that the stock trades in a narrower and narrower range, because the buying and selling pressure in the stock starts to equalize. This puts pressure on a stock like a rubber band, and when the pressure is taken out—by the sellers running out of shares to sell—the stock makes a fast move up just like a rubber band snaps back after tension is released.

Let me show you some examples.

MOV broke out of a stage one base and into a new bull market at the end of April 2003. Notice how its 200-day moving average—the red line—flattened out in the first part of 2003. The stock had resistance at $9.50 during this time and started to make higher lows right before it broke out of this period.

After this breakout, the stock entered a new bull market, during which its 200-day moving average acted as a powerful support point. Remember, this is a textbook characteristic of bull markets.

In 2003 QCOM also started a new bull market after it went through a stage one basing phase. During this basing period, $19 acted as stiff resistance. Once QCOM broke through that level, it took off like a rocket. Notice how its relative strength ratio (QCOM divided by the S&P 500) was trending up before this breakout.

Another example:

Nike Shoes—NKE—also broke into a new bull market during this time. Before it based, it had resistance at around $22.50.

Another example is Novell:

NOVL also broke out of a stage one base in 2003. It spent almost ten full months consolidating below its $4 resistance, which it broke towards the end of August and then went into a new bull market.

Right before the breakout, volume picked up heavily in NOLV. Notice how much more it went up than the other examples I have shown you so far. There is a general rule of thumb that the longer the stage one base, the bigger the bull market will be.

That rule proved itself here.

In 2003 DHI also broke out of a stage one base and entered a new bull market. You may have noticed something with these examples so far. They are all taking place at around the same time. That's because this is when the bull market of 2003-2007 began. There were hundreds of stocks that were in stage one basing phases going into the summer of 2003.

Not every year do so many stocks begin bull markets, but every year there is a sector that does, and it is best to focus on the stocks in those sectors to find ones entering new bull markets. This type of chart is best to use if you are looking to buy something as an investor with a long-term time horizon when it comes to holding on to your position. When you see several stocks in this position, then you look at valuation and earnings to decide which one is the best one to buy. I'll talk about that in a bit.

First, though, I want to give you what is really the most profitable stock pattern out there—the one that results in stocks doubling and sometimes even tripling in value quickly after you buy them. Notice that in the examples I have shown you so far, some of the stocks went up more than others after they broke out of their bases. There is a reason why.

I have found that the stocks that go up the most during their bull market phase usually start from smaller prices than their higher-priced brethren. Their stage one resistance point is at $10 or below. They also make bigger moves quickly after breaking out and go through their resistance levels with a huge volume expansion.

What I mean is that when they break out of their stage one resistance point, they have a fast and big percentage price jumps—rallying anywhere from 50% to 100%—on large volume. They then pause for one to six weeks, during which the stock goes sideways. Volatility shrinks during this time as the points of new resistance and support come closer together.

It is hard to find these stocks before they make such a big, massive break out of a stage one base. Often no one knows about them at all and they seem to just come out of nowhere unless you have a close eye on its industry and are closely watching things. But that is OK since it is during the pause after the breakout that the best buy point comes, because often stocks that double after breaking out of a stage one base pause, and then double again after they break out a second time.

Since you already have seen the stock double after breaking out of its stage one base and now are watching it consolidate, you can prepare yourself for its next big move. By rising out of the base like this, it has proven itself to be capable of making huge moves higher in a fast amount of time. And now, by pausing, it has given you a good low risk/high reward entry point to get on board as the next big rally begins.

Let me show you some examples:

For instance, VCGH broke out of a stage one base with a huge volume expansion in the summer of 2006. When it

cleared through its $1.50 resistance point, it rallied to form
new resistance at $2.50, a point 66% higher from its previ-
ous resistance point. It then paused for several weeks, and
when it broke through $2.50, it more than doubled in value
by the end of the year.

By breaking out of its stage one base with so much volume and then rallying for a 60% gain, it showed that it had
explosive momentum behind it. By then pausing for several
weeks after reaching $2.50, it would have enabled you to get
a nice, safe entry point for the next move—which turned
out to be a 100% gain. This is the most profitable stock chart
pattern that I know of.

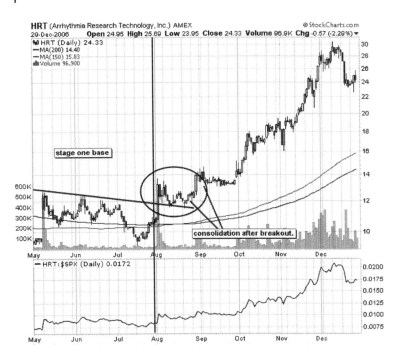

HRT formed a stage one base in the summer of 2006 with $12 as resistance. It broke $12 on high volume and then quickly jumped to the $14 area, after which it paused for another month before breaking out again and rallying over 100%.

A stock will often pause and consolidate again right after its initial breakout from a stage one base. Some people prefer not to buy stocks when they are in stage one bases or on the stage one breakout, but to instead only buy stocks that have consolidated right after the stage one breakout, because a lot of times this second consolidation period is more reliable and not all stage one breakouts have an increase in volume towards the end of them.

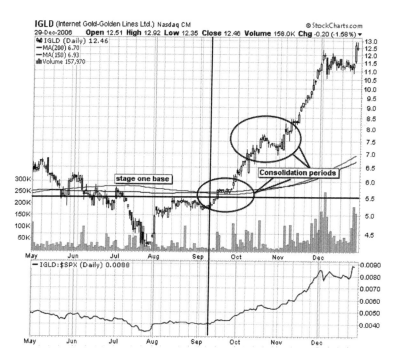

IGLD also broke out of a stage one base in the summer of 2006 in which $5.50 was resistance. After that breakout, it quickly paused, much like HRT did, before moving high up to the $7.75 area. If you missed buying before the stage one breakout, the pause would have allowed you to get in with a good entry point.

Stocks that are in bull runs will often pause several times during their bull phase, much like IGLD did when it got to $7.75. These pauses allow traders to take positions in the stocks for moves higher, but if you want to buy and hold a stock, I recommend you try to do so towards the end of a stage one base or after the first pausing period after a stock breaks out of one. Consolidations that happen later are more appropriate for short-term trading than investing or position trading.

There is an indicator that can help you spot the moment right before a stock is going to end a consolidation period and break through resistance. That indicator is the Bollinger Bands, which are the green lines in the above chart that I have set as period 10, deviation 1.5, in the chart. I don't have enough room to do a whole course on Bollinger Bands right here, but they measure the volatility in a stock.

Remember how I told you that when volatility shrinks in a stock, it happens because the selling pressure and buying pressure become more equal? That situation doesn't last forever, and when it ends by the sellers running out of stock to sell, the stock then breaks through resistance. Well, the Bollinger Bands can help you tell when this is going to happen, because when volatility increases in a stock, the two bands get farther apart, and when volatility shrinks, they come close together.

In the above chart, if you look closely you'll notice that when the stock neared the end of its consolidation period, the bands got closer together—and then the stock broke out. The bands make great advance warning indicators that an important breakthrough out of resistance is about to happen.

So far, everything I have talked with you about is looking at price and volume patterns to figure out when a sector is entering a bull market and when a stock is poised to make a large move higher. The goal isn't to guess bottoms, but to buy after the smart money has moved in and stabilized a stock by accumulating shares during the stage one basing phase. It takes the smart money to take a stock through a stage one base and into a stage two bull market, and by looking for these patterns, you can invest along with the smart money as a stock begins a new, extended bull phase.

I suggest that you go look at a list of the top-gaining stocks of the past few months and see if you can see these patterns in them. If you do this, you'll learn a lot. These are the types of stocks I like to buy myself, and in my trading service I do my best to find them for you.

When you get good at finding these stocks, you'll be able to buy into stocks with low risk/high reward entry points. However, there are also ways to figure out how high a stock may go so you can get a good idea of its potential before you buy it, and that involves some simple, fundamental analysis.

CHAPTER 8:

BUYING A STOCK USING THE TWO FOLD FORMULA

Very few people know about the things you have read about so far. They don't know how to identify a stock or sector that is about to start a new bull market. However, they know they want to buy something at a low level and see it go up. As a result, they try to buy stocks that were once high and are now falling in the hopes that they will go back up, or they get mesmerized with the idea of buying a stock that is trading at a low price. Instead of investing, they fall into speculation and news chasing.

Some try to gamble in penny stocks. Back when I first started to buy gold stocks, I started to go to gold investment conferences. At these conferences, many micro-cap gold exploration stocks would buy booths and give presentations to promote themselves. These companies were in the business of drilling for gold and precious metals on properties all over the world. Very few of these companies would be able to actually mine the metal if they discovered it, because it can easily cost tens of millions of dollars to construct a mine, but if they found a viable deposit they could partner up with a large mining company or get bought out by one. The shares of exploration stocks that did this could see their shares go from pennies to $10 or more.

Those types of returns attracted people to these stocks. However, it is so difficult to discover a viable deposit that can be mined that only one out of a thousand of these companies succeed in doing so. These companies need to raise no more than a few million dollars to do business, so they often go to private investors for financing. Wall Street tends to shun them. That is why they need investor conferences and newsletter writers for exposure.

On one hand, this is a good thing for a small investor. You can make contacts with the leaders of the gold industry, and most gold companies are very compliant with individual investors. This is a virtual impossibility in more mainstream sectors. You would have a difficult time trying to meet Bill Gates or Steve Jobs at an investment conference, but you can meet some of the biggest mining CEOs at the right conference.

On the other hand, many tiny gold companies are nothing but pieces of paper, and their reliance on small newsletter writers for exposure is a sign of their lack of investment merit. In fact, many of them border on being outright frauds. When I started to go to investment conferences that featured gold companies, I made it a point to have private conversations with the gold CEOs to get a better feel for the industry. I spent one night with one of them on a million-dollar yacht watching football and drinking beer. Loose lips are more revealing.

I didn't have a position in this man's company and don't now. I took a liking to this guy and he seemed straight to me. Of course he believed that gold would go up, but he warned me that 80% of the small cap exploration companies are "fake." He had a fifteen-year background in the industry and knew most of the key players. I asked him who the small investors can rely on. The analysts don't follow the stocks, so all you have are newsletter writers. He laughed and said that most of them are bought off with stock. He told me of one or two that were good, but then added, "You need to understand that they need to make a living."

He went on to tell me that when it comes to exploration companies, it is all about promotion. His words made comments that I heard from another CEO of a small exploration company earlier that day bounce in my head. During a conversation with this man, he made a comment to the effect that gold companies are the best companies to run, because the balance sheet doesn't matter. Earnings don't matter. People don't know how to value your properties, and it is all about their unknown potential and the "psychology" of gold.

The last time I heard CEOs say that their earnings didn't matter was during the Internet mania. Those stocks flew and crashed to nothing. When the gold bull market ends one day, most of the small cap gold stocks will go back to nothing, too.

I got the impression from both men that stock promotion is central to the junior and gold exploration stocks. The man on the yacht point blank told me that it is not the shares of companies with good resources that go up the most, but the ones with the heaviest promotion that do. The way he put it was, if you have good properties and no promotion, the stock will lag, but if you have crap properties and heavy promotion, it will fly as gold goes higher. And if you have both, then you have a rocket.

The easiest way for people to promote a gold stock is to get newsletter writers involved, especially those that specialize in the gold market. They are the people who can directly reach potential investors. Promoters get them involved by allowing them to buy stock at steep discounts on the private market, paying them money, or by simply giving them shares.

One of the most popular ways to promote a stock is to send out mass mail flyers to investors. These fliers almost always will feature a newsletter writer, who supposedly has earned his subscribers unbelievable profits, and a write-up for the company that its stock should go up 1000% or even more. That write-up is the real purpose of the mailing. The newsletter writer is just there to give it credibility.

The problem is that, more often than not, the investor who buys on these mailings is buying in near a top. The promoter, the newsletter writer, and everyone else involved in pumping the stock already got in way before the flier was sent out. After the last sucker gets in, the stock always goes back down. With no earnings or real prospects, it has nowhere else to go.

Now this isn't peculiar just to the gold world, but is typical of penny stocks in general. A few months after I talked with these people, I was driving down the road to meet some people and play golf when my cell phone rang. The guy who answered said he was on the inside of a penny stock resort company that just needed some exposure.

I had no idea who he was or how he got my phone number, but he offered me right then $20,000 if I would just recommend the stock to my readers. I told him I don't do that.

He offered me $30,000. I said no again, and he sounded as if he didn't believe me. He seemed to think that I was just trying to get him to offer me more money. So he did.

He offered me $50,000. I told him to go to hell and hung up the phone on him. I really don't like it when some random person calls me on my cell phone. They may be the worst inventions ever. Nor do I need to risk my reputation and sacrifice my integrity. I'm also not in the stock market just for the money. To me it's a fun game that brings out my competitive nature and that just happens to be measured by money. I also enjoy writing and helping people. Take the two together and it makes for a fun lifestyle, and I'm not going to risk it for something stupid.

When I got home I put his stock symbol on my monitor. I watched it for about six weeks, and every single day it dropped. Finally I took it off the screen.

This is what happens with most penny stocks. They drop! So don't get involved with them unless you really know something. If you subscribe to a newsletter or get a flyer in the mail that recommends a penny stock, read the disclaimer carefully. If the person is being paid to promote the stock, they have to put it in there or else they can go to prison. A few newsletter writers are on the up and up when it comes to penny stocks, but you have to be careful about most of the ones that you deal with.

The point is, just because a stock has a low price doesn't mean it's a bargain. Companies can go bankrupt, and stocks do go to zero at times. However, you can buy in at a low price not by guessing bottoms or buying penny stocks, but by getting in after a stock has bottomed and then stabilized just before it starts a new stage one bull market. Even then, it is helpful if you know how to value a stock using some simple fundamental analysis. When you combine these two ideas, you have what I call the Two Fold Formula to picking stocks.

You want to buy low and sell high. To know if a stock is cheap, you first have to understand some simple valuation metrics. The valuation of a stock is calculated by taking all of the shares outstanding and then multiplying that by the price. This will give you the stock's market capitalization. So, for instance, if a stock has 100 million shares outstanding and is trading at $5 a share, then it has a market cap of $500 million.

Companies with a market cap between $200 million and $2 billion are considered to be small cap stocks, while ones with market caps between $2 billion and $10 billion are midcaps. Of course, anything above that number is a large cap, while those below $200 million are considered to be more speculative microcap companies.

Large cap companies are the type of companies that are household names and make up the Dow and S&P 500. They tend to be fully mature companies, and the best of them are considered "blue chip" stocks. They make up the bulk of mutual fund holdings.

Small cap and midcap stocks are generally considered to be riskier, but the right stocks in this valuation range can go up tremendously if they are in the right sector and represent companies with fast earnings growth. As a general rule of thumb, the smaller the market cap, the more volatile and riskier a stock can be. For every successful startup company that goes from small cap to midcap and beyond, there are hundreds of companies that fail to execute, with many going broke and disappearing from the stock exchanges. However, the homework it takes to pick out quality small and midcap stocks is well worth the effort, because they are the stocks that end up on the list of top performing stocks every year.

Now it is important to know how much a stock is valued at when compared to the value of the company it represents to know if you are paying a high price for the stock or a low price, and how much potential the stock has to go up in value. Most people think that investing in stocks means either being a value or a growth investor. Value investors look for stocks that are priced at a valuation below that of the worth of the underlying company, while many growth investors do not worry about valuation at all and just look for companies with fast earnings growth.

You can combine both strategies by looking at some key valuation metrics to get the best of both situations and buy stocks that have the most potential—stocks of growth companies priced incredibly low. When it comes to valuing stocks in regards to company earnings, the most common metric used is the price-to-earnings ratio. P/E ratios are calculated by taking the price of a stock and dividing it by the earnings per share that the company generates in a year.

So, for instance, if GE were priced at $20 a share and made $2 a share, you would take 20 and divide it by 2 to get a P/E of 10.

From 1920 to 1990, the P/E of the S&P 500 has traded between 10 and 20 except for some brief periods of extreme undervaluation and overvaluation. However, it is common to find companies trading with P/Es below and above this level, because companies that are growing earnings at a fast rate often have higher P/E ratios than companies that are not. Since 1900 the average P/E of a stock has been 14. Normally when a stock has a P/E less than 10, either it is extremely undervalued or the company's earnings are in decline. Between 10 and 17 is considered a normal valuation, while stocks with a P/E between 17 and 25 are either overvalued or the company's earnings are growing fast enough to justify the larger valuation. Once you get to stocks with P/Es over 25 you are often looking at stocks that are richly valued and have become fads.

I like to use the forward P/E and PEG (P/E to growth) ratio to figure out the potential for growth stocks I own or may buy. The forward P/E divides the price by next year's annual earnings estimates to get an idea of how much potential a stock has to rise over the next year. I look for a forward P/E less than 10 to find a bargain growth stock and consider the 14 area as my target valuation. So if a stock has a forward P/E of 7, I consider it as having the potential to double in price over the next twelve months based on earnings growth. Of course, it can go up more than that if enough investors get excited about it, which happens a lot in bull markets with growth stocks, but once a stock I own goes from having a small bargain forward P/E to reaching the 14 level, I consider it fairly valued from a valuation standpoint.

Famous investors Peter Lynch and John Templeton used the PEG ratio to do a similar type of analysis. The PEG ratio divides the P/E by the expected earnings growth rate for the next five years. Both considered growth stocks to be fully valued at a PEG ratio of 1.0 and stocks below that to have the potential to move higher, with the lower the ratio, the better. Templeton, for instance, would look to buy stocks with PEG ratios below 0.50. If a stock has a forward P/E of 14 and a low PEG ratio, this is because analysts are projecting high earnings growth for years out. Such a stock may still be cheaply valued.

I also look at the PEG ratios for stocks that I own or am looking at as potential buy candidates. You can find the P/E and PEG ratios for your stocks by going to Yahoo! Finance, typing in the ticker symbol, and then hitting the link for Key Statistics on the left sidebar. You also can scan for stocks in the whole market with low PEG ratios and other valuation metrics by using their stock screening tool. You can find it by hitting Investing on the top navigation bar of Yahoo! Finance and then clicking stocks.

However, when I look for stocks to buy, I normally do sector analysis first, then look for stocks that have the chart patterns I already went over with you, and then look at these earnings ratios last to get an idea of how much potential a stock has to rise according to valuation metrics. This is usually the last piece of analysis I do, because it is always the price action that is the most important variable. Nonetheless, I often use these metrics to narrow down a list of potential buy candidates. Given a choice between two stocks with identical price action and growth characteristics, I would rather choose the one with the smallest PEG ratio and forward P/E.

If you use the technical price patterns I have taught you with these valuation metrics, than you can find stocks that are truly cheap in value and poised to go up. You will have no need to speculate in penny stocks or get caught up in hype ever again. This will give you the best chance of building solid returns, because it is based on real investment methodologies practiced by some of the most successful investors who have ever lived.

CHAPTER 9:
MANAGE YOUR RISK

Imagine this scenario. You are the CEO of a giant airline company. You have invested $100 million of the company's money into a research project, the purpose of which is to build an airplane that cannot be detected by conventional radar. When the plane is 90% completed, a competitor begins marketing a plane that cannot be detected by any radar. It also is much faster and far more economical than the plane your company is building. Do you invest the final remaining 10% of your research funds to finish your plane?

If you answered yes, than you have made a big mistake. You have literally thrown good money down what has now become an investment trap. Don't feel bad if you did say yes, because the economists who created this survey found that 85% of the people who answered it said they would, too.

However, when they changed the question so that it did not mention any prior investments, only 17% said they would keep spending money on the project.[1]

From a purely financial standpoint, there is no logical reason to spend the remaining $10 million, because the airplane is going to be useless in the face of your competitor's plane. The research project is now a waste of money. The commitment already made to the project, though, prevents most people from walking away from it, even though that is the right thing to do.

What is really at issue is not the money, but the feelings people have about making mistakes and taking losses. If they walk away from the project, they may feel that they have lost $90 million on it or, at the very least, have made a mistake. By continuing the project, they escape from these feelings of loss or disappointment by putting them off. They may also fool others and themselves into believing that everything is fine.

This type of behavior is natural to people and can cause them to lose fortunes in the stock market. There is an old adage that you make money trading by letting winners run and cutting losers, but most people have a very difficult time doing this. In fact, they tend to do the opposite by holding on to losing positions until they get so upset that they cannot take the losses anymore and then selling them while they cut their winning positions short to make up for their losing trades and in fear that they will become losers, too.

When people make an investment, they make a commitment and they buy into an idea that it will make them

---

1. Scott Plous, *The Psychology of Judgment and Decision Making* (New York: McGraw-Hill, 1993), p. 244.

money. It is as if they bought a lottery ticket that they never rub the numbers off of. As long as they don't look to see whether their ticket is a winner or loser, they can fantasize about the money it might make them.

Most people treat the stock market like this. If they buy into a stock and it drops, they don't get out because they fear that if they sell out at a loss, they will feel like a loser. They associate selling for a loss with making a mistake and being wrong. They also convince themselves that as long as they hold on, things might turn around and make them rich.

These feelings are so powerful for people that most will take bigger risks to prevent losses than they will to actually make money. Do you remember the story about the lady who doubled down on her losing positions in the stock market using a credit card? She risked more than she even had to try to prevent taking the losses.

You have got to cut losing positions if you are going to consistently make money in the stock market. There is no other way around this. Say you evenly put your money into ten stocks and one of them went to zero. That one stock would mean an overall loss of 10% for your whole account. Do that a few times and you've created a tough wall to climb back over. In a bear market, you can easily see all of your stocks fall in value.

The good news is that if you cut your losing positions and hold your winning positions, all it takes is a few big winners to make a huge return, because you can easily see a few of your stocks double in value or go up even more if you just hold on to them. Just managing your money properly can make you big money even if you don't pick out stocks well. If just half go up and make you money and you cut your losing positions properly, you can still come out way ahead.

But most people simply can't get past their ego. The problem is that people tend to react to the feelings they have about the here and now and do not really look forward properly when it comes to managing their investments. Selling a single stock for a loss does not make you a loser. It is completely mismanaging your money that does.

People have a tendency to rationalize holding on to losers by coming up with excuses. In a study of football gamblers, economists found that their comments indicated that they spend more time talking about losses than wins and talked about them in a different manner. The bettors tended to make comments that "undid" the losses by chalking them up to wild flukes. They explained away their losses and took full responsibility for their winners. [2]

When it comes to the stock market, people tend to do the same thing by blaming their falling positions on forces outside of their control, such as bad luck, market makers, a random news event, or stock market manipulators while reasoning that their winning positions are due to their remarkable foresight. What they do is take responsibility for their winning trades but none for their losing positions.

This is a game for adults, not children. To be a true winner in the stock market, you have to take full responsibility for your money and your own decisions. Let's not be too hard on people, though, because one reason most do not do this is because they simply do not know any better.

Whenever you buy a stock, you can enter a stop loss order to sell it if it falls below a certain price. If you just do this every time you buy a stock, you will automatically cut

---

2. Gary Belsky and Thomas Gilovich, *Why Smart People Make Big Money Mistakes* (New York: Simon and Schuster, 1999), p. 55.

out of any losing positions before they could become big losses. It is easy if you just know where to put the stop loss orders.

Some people argue against stop losses. They say that if you use them, then all you will do is get shaken out of your positions, because if you set a 15% or 20% stop loss order and the stock drops that far, you have no idea whether it will continue to fall or if it will just turn around there. They are right in a sense that you cannot use a rigid, fixed percentage for all of your stop loss orders.

If you do you will often end up selling for losses only to have things go right back after you sell, which is one of the greatest fears that people have. Instead, all you have to do is just use stop loss orders the right way. What I do is when I buy a stock I look at its stock chart to determine where its most recent support level is and I put my stop right under there.

If the stock were to go through that support level, it would mean that the trend that I was betting on was no longer valid. I do not want to be buying, much less holding, stocks that are going into a new trend of falling prices. That's how you lose money. So I place my stop loss orders at a point where, if a stock fell to that level, I would be very concerned and would want to get out.

Then, once I figure out where I want to put my stop loss order, I take a look at where the stock is trading now. I figure out how many points of difference are between these two prices to figure out how much money I am willing to put in this stock. So sometimes I may have a stop loss order just 5% away and other times it could be as far as 10% away, depending on how far away its support level is from my entry point.

I then look to see how high I expect the stock price to go up. Comparing the number of points I stand to risk to what I stand to gain gives me an idea of the risk-to-reward ratio I am really playing with. Generally speaking, you want to be risking $1 for every $3 you make in the stock market. If you make trades that consistently do this, you will make a huge amount of money even if half the trades somehow don't work out.

When you start to think like this about your trading, you won't get caught up in worrying about the effects of every single trade you make and getting obsessed with the idea that every trade has to be a winner or that you will be a failure. In fact, you won't feel like that at all, because instead of letting the gyrations of individual stocks control your feelings, you will feel confident about your own knowledge and investment abilities. As you make more money, you will create a positive feedback loop for yourself that will make you feel like a true winner in the stock market, no matter what happens with an individual trade.

Most people think that stock trading is extremely stressful and that to be good at it, you need to be mentally tough and somehow push aside or block out the feelings of anxiety that it brings. But in reality this isn't true at all. They simply are approaching the stock market in a way that does create anxiety, because they are investing and trading like a pure gambler. Once you trade with a strategy that works and manages risk, then you don't feel anxious at all. Instead you will invest with confidence. You'll find that stock trading will be as much of a sure thing as possible for you.

Your real goal in the stock market is to put your money into the best stocks possible. Of course, not every stock you buy is going to meet this lofty objective, and at times there will be some new stocks that come along and provide you with an even better opportunity to make money than something you may already own does. When you buy a stock and it gets stopped out for a loss, this doesn't make you a loser or some sort of failure. What it does is free up that money so that you can put it to use in a new position with more potential than that one had. And having your money moving into the best places to be is what investing is all about.

You may be wondering how many stocks you should buy. Now I can't tell you how much of your portfolio should go into individual stocks, exchange trade funds, mutual funds, bonds, commodities, or other investments. How you diversify your money has to do with how much experience you have and how much risk you're willing to take and feel comfortable with, not to mention the current market trends. It is an individual matter. So let's just talk about what to do with the money you are allocating to individual stocks.

There is no one perfect answer that works for everyone. As a rule of thumb, the more stocks you buy, the less benefit you will have from being right with your big winners, but the fewer you buy the more at risk you are to have one stock blow a hole in your portfolio. So you do want to be spread out in several issues. But really ten is probably enough to be well-enough diversified so that one stock blowing up won't hurt you too much.

A little more is better if you have a lot of money to invest with. I like to do fifteen to twenty stocks when I am fully invested in stock positions. I don't really see the point to having more than that unless you have so much money that you need more positions due to liquidity reasons.

One thing you do not want to do is own so many stocks that you cannot keep up with what is happening with them.

You will want to chart out your stocks on a weekly basis and see if there are any developments with them. Set alerts on them to let you know if something happens that warrants your immediate attention. Most brokers will let you set up alerts when price points are reached or news comes out on a stock, and these alerts can be e-mailed to you or sent to your phone. You don't want to own so many stocks that you are overwhelmed with this type of information.

It is also best to be spread out in a few stock sectors so not all of your stocks are linked to the rise and fall of one industry group. Unless you have a small account and are swinging for the fences like I was when I started out, I would not put more than 20% of your money into one single stock either.

You'll find out from experience what the best number of stocks to buy is for you. You'll find out how many you want to keep up with and how much money makes you comfortable to put into them. If you feel worried about them, then you know it is too much. Then just do less. It's that simple. You do not want to be a slave to your stocks, but to have your stocks work for you.

CHAPTER 10:
UNDERSTAND INVESTMENT CROWD PSYCHOLOGY

Several years ago I was presented with a money-making opportunity that would have made Charles Ponzi proud. I was out visiting some local small businesspeople I know when they told me about a "gifting" pyramid scheme they had just gotten into. All you had to do was put down $2,000 to get in it.

In return you got a sheet of paper with boxes drawn on it—some empty and some filled in with names—aligned in a pyramid structure. You could make back $16,000 if you recruited two more people into it who themselves succeeded in recruiting two more people who recruited two more people. Once you got paid, you would move off the sheet of paper and those people below you would move up.

I knew that such a scheme could not continue forever, because as more people joined, more and more people would be needed to recoup any money invested. As soon as there were no more people left to get in, it would collapse. I thought that it might be early enough that one could make money, but there is no way it would last forever. Despite being told about some big-money men that were in it, and even a few people connected to local politicians and city officials, I wanted no part of it.

A day went by and I heard nothing more about it. Then I heard a few people talk about it. Some asked me if I thought they should get in. They were worried that it might be a scam, but they heard stories of big-name people who had gotten paid out. Someone heard of a car dealership where money was piled on a table and people were coming in and picking it up. Supposedly dozens of workers at a Goodyear tire plant were making money off of it.

Then, all of a sudden, the next day I got several more phone calls from people asking me if they should get in. That night I went out to dinner and had a dozen people come up to me and ask me if I wanted to get in. It was amazing, because it was almost as if people were coming up to me every five minutes. All of them were already in it.

I'd just shake my head at them, telling I just couldn't do it. So many people talking about it meant that it had to be almost over. I couldn't tell them how sorry I felt for them. The next morning the newspaper ran a story on the front page about the pyramid scheme. And of course it totally collapsed. I'm sure a few people made a lot of money off of it, but the vast majority of people who got caught up in the excitement now faced shame and humiliation for losing their heads.

The psychology of stock market moves is very similar to a pyramid scheme. Stock market rallies are fueled by buying and continue as long as more people buy into the market. At first as a market starts to go up, most people hesitate to buy in. But eventually as they see the market go higher and higher, they fear missing out, so they buy in.

At some point all of the people out there that are potential buyers buy into the market. Then, once there is no one left to buy, the market rally comes to an end and a correction begins. This is how all short-term rallies end, how bull markets end, and even how upward moves in individual stocks come to an end.

This is what truly fuels market moves. What is fascinating is that investor psychology is closely correlated to major tops and bottoms in the market. What happens is that most people, when they have a heavy cash position, feel uncertain or cautious about the market. They may even be bearish on the market, thinking it is too risky to buy. What they are not is bullish on the market. If they were, they would buy into it.

But once they do buy into the market, they become bullish on the market and start to accept bullish arguments and theories for why the stock market will continue higher. As more and more people buy into the market, surveys that poll market participants show that the number of people who consider themselves bullish on the market increases.

This is why at major tops almost everyone is bullish on the stock market and investor sentiment surveys often record an unusually high number of people as being bullish on the market. The problem is, when everyone is bullish, everyone is in, and soon there will be no one left to buy any more shares.

During big declines, the opposite happens with investor psychology. As a decline begins most people just hold on, thinking that the decline is temporary, and they remain bullish on the market. But once someone fears that the market will just keep going lower, he or she sells out and become a bear on the market. As more and more people sell, the number of bears grows, and at a major stock market bottom, bearish sentiment becomes widespread. Often it grows to the point where true panic can strike.

Bullish and bearish trends can last for years, so most of the time the vast majority of investors can be on the right side of the trend. But at key tops and bottoms, the masses are always wrong, and those critical moments make and break fortunes. That is why it pays to separate yourself from the crowd.

Investors tend to move in a herd, and when everyone starts to think alike, then watch out. In fact, during bear markets, you have to watch out in order to survive, because almost everyone stays bullish until the end of a bear market, and in bull markets almost everyone remains too cautious to take advantage of them at the beginning. The real money is made by making the right decisions at these important times.

You simply cannot make the big money doing what everyone else is doing, because, truth be told, the average person actually loses money in the stock market even in bull markets. Terrance Odean, an assistant professor at the University of California, did a fascinating study of investor success rates back in the 1990s.

Odean received the trading history of over sixty thousand accounts that were active been 1991 and 1996 from a discount broker and used the data to study the trading behaviors of online investors. Most of them underperformed the stock market, and only a small minority beat the market. In fact, only half of active traders managed to just break even. Most simply made a little or lost a little. Professional investors do not fare all that much better, as half of all mutual funds fail to beat the S&P 500 index every year.

Only a small minority of individual investors produced outstanding returns. The top 5%, for instance, had an average return over 2.41% a month, and only 1% had a return over 4.86% a month. These are huge returns over the course of a year. The statistics show that a few elite investors and traders make all of the money while just about everyone else breaks even or loses.[3]

Big success in the market means having a deep understanding of investment psychology. In my view the real reason most people don't do well in the stock market is because they just follow the crowd. Instead of thinking for themselves, they buy what other people tell them to buy and believe what others tell them. They get caught up in hype and invest on emotion.

They do zero real thinking or analysis. The average man is not blessed—or cursed, however you may want to look at it—with an analytical mind. We see through a glass darkly. All of our thoughts are always enveloped in a haze from

3. Brad Barber and Terrance Odean, "Trading is Hazardous to Your Wealth: The Common Stock Investment Performance of Individual Investory," *The Journal of Finance*, April 2000.

which we find it painful if not impossible to escape. Many of our emotions and some of our acts are merely automatic responses to external stimuli.

Our haziness increases in proportion to the difficulty of the subject and our ignorance of it. From reading, observation, and conversation, most are presented with a jumble of ideas from which they conclude that the situation is bullish or bearish. If the stocks go up, they buy and listen to the bulls, and if they fall long enough and they suffer so much pain that they can't take holding anymore, they sell and become a bear.

If they are bulls, they follow the bullish stock market commentators, and if they are bearish, they follow prophets of doom, but they do very little thinking on their own. In the end, that causes them to be on the wrong side of the market at the times that it is so important for them to be completely objective and in alignment with what the stock market is really doing, instead of what they just want to believe it is doing.

The problem is, when people get into a crowd they do things that they normally would not do on their own. History proves that politicians know that crowds can be easily manipulated into doing just about anything, even killing their fellow man. When it comes to investing or money decisions, when people fall into crowd psychology they lose their sense of balance and fall for hype. They'll buy into the most outlandish penny stocks, scams, and so-called "investment opportunities." Buying into the top of a stock market rally or bull market is easy to do. As the stock market goes up higher and higher, and as more and more people buy into it, the faster bullish ideas spread.

Buying at a top actually feels like a good thing to do, because so many others are doing it and believing in the market. That's just human nature. And that is the irony of investment psychology. We can put down crowd thinking, but most of the time crowd thinking is right. How many times have you gotten off of an airplane and not looked at any signs and just followed the other passengers to the baggage area? Most of the time you don't have time to analyze every social situation, and it's easier to just follow the crowd, because it works so well in everyday life.

But investing with the crowd in the stock market does not take you to the promised land of stock market riches. But it's tough for most people to remain objective investors, because once a bullish or bearish extreme level of sentiment is reached, when you discuss your then-contrary views, most will react violently to what you tell them. Believe me—as someone who writes about the financial markets, I know this for fact.

When everyone is bullish or bearish and you decide they are wrong, you literally are fighting a majority opinion held by millions of people and trumpeted by all of the people held up as experts on Wall Street, the press, and financial television—the very people that most of the people you know look up to and obey when they make investment decisions. So if you go against these opinion leaders, you may fear that your friends will think you to be a fool and you are telling them something they probably don't want to hear and won't listen to anyway!

The only way you can prevent yourself from being influenced by the herd like everyone else is to have a real strategy for investing and a way to interpret market action that works well enough that you believe in it more than you do than what the experts tell you. This book should enable you to do this.

The funny thing is that some people argue that market-beating investment techniques and strategies, such as stock charting or technical analysis, can't work, because if they did work, everyone would use them and therefore make them lose their effectiveness. But people will never change. The vast majority of the masses are simply too lazy to truly take advantage of the stock market in the right way.

Remember, when it comes to investing, most people simply will not put in the thought or work it takes to make real money. They'd rather just throw money at the market or give some money to someone they think is an expert and hope they know what are doing than really dedicate them-selves to mastering the stock market. They confuse gambling with investing.

As you get more and more experienced in the market, you will get a better feel for the mass psychology of inves-tors and recognize the times when people are overly bear-ish or bullish about the market. You'll notice that there are times when one big market opinion or news story seems to dominate the news and people's minds.

People like to think of going against the crowd as con-trarian investing, but you don't make money by going against the consensus all of the time—only when the time is right. That means you have to keep an open mind as much as possible and be flexible in your own beliefs and willing to change them if the market actions tell you that you must. Instead of simple contrarianism, I like to think of successful investing as two-sided thinking—being willing to examine your own investment opinions and see what could happen to force you to change them.

That doesn't mean overly doubting yourself, but being prepared and staying as objective as possible. The person who makes the most money in the stock market is the one who stays most aligned with the reality of the market trends and adapts when they change.

CHAPTER 11:
ESCAPE THE WINNER'S CURSE OF INVESTING

Imagine for the moment that you have a friend that is the chairman of an oil company. He calls you for advice about a problem that has come up for him. Another oil company has gone into bankruptcy and its oil exploration properties have come up for auction. There is a plot of land that your friend is interested in bidding on during a bankruptcy auction.

He had expected two other firms to bid on this land, and your friend had intended to bid a million dollars for it. Now he has learned that five other firms have joined in the bidding, bringing the total to ten. He is wondering if he should increase his bid and asks you for his advice. What do you tell him to do?

Most people, when presented with this problem, decide to bid more, because there are now additional bidders and if you don't bid more you probably will lose out. However, what most people don't consider is this—suppose each person bidding in the auction is willing to bid just a little less than what he thinks the land is really worth. Of course, no one knows for sure how much oil is in the ground, so some bidders will guess too high while others will guess too low.

The person who wins the auction will end up being the person who is the most optimistic about the amount of oil in the ground and that person will almost always end up bidding more than the land is worth. Economists call this the winner's curse. In an auction with lots of bidders, the winning bidder often becomes an investment loser. In a situation like this, the best way to bid is to do so conservatively, and if your bid doesn't win, look for another opportunity to bid on.[4]

What really drives the person to bid high in this example is not greed, but the fear of missing out on an opportunity. This fear dominates investor psychology when it comes to the stock market, too; so much so that I think it is more useful to understand investors as being driven mainly by fear and not by greed, especially when it comes to professional investors.

I have talked one on one with investors in thousands of situations, have read who knows how many individual pieces of feedback from readers, and co-managed a hedge fund for several years. One thing I discovered is that if I have an investment idea that doesn't work out like I think it will or loses money, people do not mind much. Rarely will someone

4. Richard Thaler, *The Winner's Curse: Paradoxes and Anomalies of Economic Life* (New Jersey: Princeton University Press, 1992), p. 1.

complain. However, if I tell people to sell something and it goes up afterwards, they can get extremely angry, even if it would have been very risky to continue to hold on.

People are more fearful of missing out on a rising stock market or some investment opportunity than they are of losing money. This is one reason people just hold on during bear markets. When most people invest in a mutual fund or give their money to a stock broker or investment advisor and they end up losing money, they do not mind so much as long as the rest of the stock market goes down, too. However if the stock market goes up and their investments fail to rise as much as the market, they will get furious. They'll pull their money out of the mutual fund or call up their broker and take their money away from him.

It is almost as if people do not care if they lose money as long as they know that others are losing money with them, but they cannot stand the idea that everyone else might make money and they won't. I have never seen anyone talk about this, and most people do not even know that they think like this. Jealousy drives investors much more than greed does. It is the simple fear of missing out when others gain.

This leads to pure crowd following. If the crowd loses money and the typical investor loses money, too, the investor can at least take comfort with the crowd. But if the crowd makes money and the investor doesn't, then he'll feel alone. So he cannot separate himself from the crowd and take control of his money. But without doing this he stands virtually zero chance of becoming one of the elite few who make almost all of the money in the stock market.

You can probably think of many ways that this can impact the individual investor, but what you probably do not realize is how deep an impact this has on professional investors who give investment advice or manage other people's money. And these professionals very rarely realize how they are affected by this. Most of this stuff happens in the subconscious.

When it comes to investment writers and Wall Street analysts, reporters, and opinion makers, they often stay bullish on the stock market all of the time, because they will be punished by the masses more for being bearish and wrong about the market than they are if they are bullish and wrong. Most people simply want to hear bullish opinions all of the time, and many want them even more in bear markets for the comfort they can give them as they hold on. Investment advisors are really paid by their clients to do nothing but hold their hands.

As a result, financial news tends to be skewed to the bull side of arguments. I know of someone who was on one of the biggest financial television networks as a guest in 2000, and once he got bearish on the market and told people to sell out of tech stocks, he was never invited again. The producer actually told him that by being bearish, he was being unpatriotic.

In another instance, I know of a person who was writing for a large financial newsletter company and decided that the stock market would decline. After he wrote that, one of the top managers of the company called him and cursed him out on the phone, telling him that is not what sells newsletters, much less keeps readers. But you do not need to cater to the lowest common denominator in order to write about the stock market and have readers. I'd rather have fewer, more influential people following what I have to say then hundreds of thousands of losers.

People will often behave and believe in the ways that they are incentivized to do so. This is more true than you can imagine on Wall Street. A stockbroker has all of the incentive in the world to tell his client what he thinks his client wants to hear, and very little incentive to actually save a client from a bear market.

It is a huge risk for a broker or investment advisor to tell a client to get out of the market, because if the market goes up afterwards, the client will almost certainly take his money away from that broker. If the broker convinces the client to get out and the market falls, the client will be happy, but he will rarely be thankful—while if the client holds on during a bear market with the broker's encouragement, the typical client won't care, because he'll just think the market is falling for some fluke reason and everyone else is losing money anyway.

So the money manager has every incentive to remain bullish all of the time. This is why almost all money managers fail to protect their clients in bear markets. The thing is, most do not even know that they behave in this manner. They are trained to do this, and very few of them possess the knowledge to know any better and it doesn't pay them to do better.

Most money managers are confidence men who put on a bull face while inside they suffer from extreme self-doubt and lack of confidence in themselves, because they know very little about how the stock market really works, much less what it might do. There are a handful of investment advisors and brokers that I have met over the years that are truly knowledgeable and have done an incredible job helping their clients, but in all of these cases, their clients have no idea how fortunate they are to be working with such a person.

Mutual funds are structured in a way to simply invest on the long side of the market all of the time. This is why, whenever you see a mutual fund manager interviewed on TV, he is almost always bullish on the stock market. When it comes to hedge funds, they are usually evaluated on a monthly basis by their investors and by large Wall Street institutions that invest in them. This sets the hedge fund manager in a high-pressure situation where he needs to beat the market every single month, which is almost impossible for anyone to do—maybe you can do it every year, but not every month.

Over the past few years so much money has flowed into hedge funds that they have come to have a large influence on the stock market. This has caused the stock market to trade in a much more volatile manner than it has in the past, because hedge fund managers are forced to focus on the short-term moves of the stock market in their quest to post superior performance numbers every single month.

Even more so than an individual investor, hedge fund managers are driven by a huge fear of missing out on rallies, since it can not only cost them their ego, but their livelihood, too. This can cause them to buy in at tops and, since they do not know how to manage risk, make it so that when the market does top out, it can be prone to quick and violent corrections, which in the past did not occur as frequently as they do now.

In this book I have given you some strategies that I use to make money in the stock market, including an easy method to identify the large trends of the market and ways to pick out stocks that have the best chance to provide outstanding returns. However, I have also spent a lot of time discussing the psychological aspects of investing and trading with you, probably more than you expected when you first opened up this book.

I have done this because I believe they are the truly critical components to investing, and I talk about them from experience. The mistakes I talk about people making are ones that I have made myself. I have come to conclude that what it takes to become a top trader in the market is to learn from your mistakes. Most people's egos simply prevent them from being honest enough with themselves about their investment results and why they have them. Therefore they never learn.

I told you that when I first started out in the stock market, I read many books and learned many strategies that I thought would work in the market but failed to use a real strategy until I was forced to. Taking responsibility for your results leads to learning and eventually money making, which, with enough time, will lead to what I call strategic stock trading—trading with full confidence because you have a method that works and are as objective on the market as you can possibly be. You then invest with peace of mind.

The most important thing when it comes to making money in the stock market is how you approach trading; how you think about your results and how well you understand and face the different pressures that impact everyone who tries his hand at investing. Most never think of these things, but it is those who do that end up becoming super stock traders. It is your attitude that counts.

Most people are under the mistaken impression that Wall Street is full of winners, but it's not. It is actually easier for you as an individual investor to make money in the stock market, because you are not under the pressures of the money manager or professional trader, hedge fund manager, or mutual fund manager that cause them to make investment mistakes.

You don't have to worry about missing out on every rally in the market or trying to beat the market with a shortened time horizon of every single month. You can take a longer-term view of things and stay focused on the big trends of the market. This is very difficult for the professional money manager to really do. I know because I found it to be a struggle myself to manage other people's money. It is one of the reasons I got out of the hedge fund business and have no interest in managing other people's money.

The fear of missing out on a market move often causes people to trade when they shouldn't. To really make good investments, you have to be patient at times to wait for good opportunities to line up. This fear of missing out will cause someone who should know better to buy in at a top instead of waiting for a short-term pullback or a good entry point in a stock.

It can easily cause you to make a trade before you should or make trades just for the sake of trading. Most of the people who sign up for one of my premium investment or trading services will stay for years, but about 10% of the people will cancel within the first two months. Sometimes someone will cancel in forty-eight hours. The number one reason they give for doing this is that they simply want more stock trades.

I personally try to only make trades when I think there is a big opportunity to make money. Sometimes this means

I'll make many trades within a short period of time, and then there may be months when I just hold my positions or don't make any trades, especially during a market decline or bear market. The people who run most trading services don't even actually own the stocks they recommend or make the trades they talk about. They simply sell people a constant stream of trading ideas, because that is what the masses want. They just want and crave action. What I want is high-probability winners where you stand to make much more than you risk.

I do the trades I talk about and invest in the stocks I discuss, too. Despite making it clear to people that I'm not about giving you trades just to do it, because this is for real, a few people can't wait a few days much less a few weeks and just cancel out. They don't read any of my educational materials and seem to just think that you can make money by putting a trade on at any moment. I do not see how these people can ever make any money in the stock market, because they just don't have the patience to do so, which is a big requirement.

Unfortunately, being patient is a tough thing for most people to do, because everywhere you look there is some-one or something pulling you in to do a trade. It could be a paid tout recommending some penny stock. It could be someone on TV calling for a big bottom or rally or simply the stock ticker itself. But there are times when it is best to stand aside and do nothing but hold what you have or wait in cash. You have to have the discipline to sit tight during those times. Remember, investing in the stock market is a marathon and not a slot machine.

CHAPTER 12:
HOLD A CORE POSITION

If you asked me what is the most important thing when it comes to successful investing, I would have to tell you that the one thing you need to do is to position yourself in alignment with the big trend of the market. This means that in bear markets you don't try to guess bottoms as the market keeps falling, but instead remain cautious and patient as you look forward to positioning yourself after the bear market is over in new sectors that will lead the next bull market. Of course, to do that will require you to push aside almost all of the advice you get from the financial media in regards to the stock market during bear markets and to not get lured in to the siren song of trading just to try to make something happen.

This may sound like common sense to you right now. A lot of trading maxims that people say do sound like common sense, and they are. Take the phrase "buy low and sell high," for example. But very few people can actually put these ideas into practice, because they simply follow the crowd. That is why I have spent so much time talking to you about psychological factors when it comes to investing and understanding exactly how the masses handle their money.

In sideways markets that come after a bear market bottom, this means remaining relatively cautious, too. Sideways markets have a habit of causing people to churn their money over as they buy too early into temporary tops in the market. They get fooled into thinking that the false rallies that create them represent the start of a brand new bull market, and then sell as the market scarily turns back down and tests support and shakes them out of their positions—just as the smart money uses these dips to accumulate stocks at cheap prices.

Sideways markets cause wild emotional swings of hope and despair in the people who get fooled by these movements, because they focus too much attention on the daily and weekly gyrations of the stock market instead of the big picture, which is the long trend of the market that you now know how to analyze by looking at the market's overall price pattern and its position relative to its long-term 150 and 200-day moving averages. If the market is below these moving averages and they are pointing down, then you are in a bear market. If they are acting as support, then you are witnessing a bull market. But if they are going sideways, then you know for sure that the market is in a sideways pattern itself.

Now in a bull market in which a market or sector is in a powerful stage two uptrend and is in a position in which it is not only above its 150 and 200-day long-term moving averages, but those moving averages are sloping upwards and acting as support, you want to buy on dips back down to the moving averages. You also want to get in as early in the bull market as possible and invest in a core position to hold.

Most people don't get in a bull market early. Instead they doubt it as it starts to go up and then buy in near a top. Few can get in just as it starts, because few understand how to use the things I have taught you to figure out. They can't tell what the real long-term trend of the market is and when it changes. All they focus on is what the market does today and the daily news stories.

You want to buy at the start of a bull market by buying when a market nears the end of a stage one sideways basing pattern that comes after a bear market or shortly after a market completes this sideways phase and begins a new bull market. You'll know a bull market is just beginning when the long-term moving averages have been going sideways for months and the market finally has a sustainable rally above these moving averages. Then you'll want to buy the first dip back down to them, or buy into strong relative strength sectors and stocks that are in the process of breaking out into new bull markets themselves. Not everything goes up at all once in a new bull market, so you do not have to worry about missing out. Some sectors start their bull markets later.

To fully take advantage of a bull market, though, you need to hold a core position from the start of the bull market to you near its end, or until it's clear to you that the bull market is over. You don't need to buy at the exact bottom or sell at the exact top to make a huge amount of money. If you get in early enough, you'll get in lots of sectors and stocks that double or triple in value. Some can even go up much more than that. The trick is to hold the best of your positions through the duration of a bull market.

Imagine having bought Apple at $10 a share and then holding it for six years as it goes to $250 a share. Or buying Google after it went public for less than $100 and then seeing it go to $700. One of the hardest things to do is to hold in a bull market, because it is so easy to get shaken out or get scared over some news story.

I know this the hard way. I bought gold stocks in 2002 when the XAU gold stock index was around $65. I traded in and out of gold stocks and made a lot of money on the swings, but I would have done better overall if I had put a percentage of my money into a core position and held that, too.

What makes it so tough to hold in a bull market is that all bull markets are prone to quick pullbacks and corrections that can cause you to lose a lot of your profits. That's not fun when it happens, so it is extremely tempting to try to trade in and out. If you are a great trader you can do this with some success, but you still have to fight the fact that you are going to have to pay higher taxes than you would if you had just held, and if at some point your trading doesn't go perfectly, you may get shaken out of the bull market and miss out on some big gains.

There is a great story about this in the biography of Jesse Livermore, *Reminiscences of a Stock Operator*. In case you don't know who Livermore is, he was the greatest trader of the first half of the twentieth century, amassing just as much personal wealth as the famous hedge fund traders and investors of today like Warren Buffett and George Soros have. After the 1929 stock market crash, he was worth $100 million dollars, which would be worth about $1.2 billion today. He didn't do this by managing other people's money or taking fees, but by trading his own personal account, thereby making this accomplishment even more impressive.

In his biography there is a great story of a character he calls Partridge, who is an old, wise trader that a bunch of younger traders in a trading house look up to. At the time, whenever someone would ask him what do about a stock, all he would answer is "You know, it's a bull market," as if that were all one needed to know.

He gives a tip to an Elmer Harwood for Climax Motors. The stock goes up, and one day Harwood comes into the office to tell Partridge that he had just sold his stock, because "the market is entitled to a reaction and I'll be able to buy it back cheaper. So you'd better do likewise."

Partridge still has the stock and refuses to sell, because "this is a bull market!" If he sells now he fears that he will only lose his position. "When you are as old as I am," he explains, "and you've been through as many booms and panics as I have, you'll know that to lose your position is something nobody can afford; not even John D. Rockefeller. I hope the stock reacts and that you will be able to repurchase your line at a substantial concession, sir. But I myself can only trade in accordance with the experience of many years. I paid a high price for it and I don't feel like throwing away a second tuition fee. But I am as much obliged to you as if I had the money in the bank. It's a bull market, you know."

This was one of the biggest lessons that Livermore learned. According to Livermore, "What old Mr. Partridge said did not mean much to me until I began to think about my own numerous failures to make as much money as I ought to when I was so right on the general market. The more I studied, the more I realized how wise that old chap was. He had evidently suffered from the same defect in his young days and knew his own human weaknesses. He would not lay himself open to a temptation that experience had taught him was hard to resist and had always proved expensive to him, as it was to me."

What this means is that you don't just buy and hold and then never look again, but instead stay aligned with the longer-term trends of the market and adapt only when it changes. Partridge held because it was a bull market, not because he just holds no matter what. All that mattered to him was whether it was a bull market or a bear market. That is the key.

"I think it was a long step forward," Livermore continued, "in my trading education when I realized at last that when old Mr. Partridge kept on telling the other customers, 'Well, you know this is a bull market!' he really meant to tell them that the big money was not in the individual fluctuations but in the main movements—that is, not in reading the tape but in sizing up the entire market and its trend."

The truth is, it is simply human nature to focus on the here and now and not be patient and forward looking. All of the news you hear about the stock market is always focused on this instant and not the big trends and where they are really carrying the market. The simple fact of the matter is that thousands are influenced every single day by the hourly gyrations of the market to commit huge investment blunders.

The in-your-face hourly market movements and constant stream of breaking financial news stories give you a distorted view of what really is happening in the stock market and cause you to miss the forest for the trees. If you want to make the big money from the big trends, then you may be best to stay away from the financial news and the stock ticker, for the ticker watcher is no more capable of well-reasoned decisions than someone who is on an acid trip. You see the daily price actions produce a mental intoxication in people.

To watch a stock hour by hour after you buy it is one of the most foolish things you can do. To watch it go down is certainly no fun, but to watch it go up when it doesn't need watching does you no good either. The time to watch is before you buy. In order to control your risk after you buy, all you need to do is put in a stop loss order and just check back every couple of days or so. Watching it tick by tick won't prevent it from going down if that is what it is going to do.

If you cannot stop yourself from doing this, then you need to realize that you are not really in the stock market to make money, but are in the stock market to feel the excitement that the act of trading brings you. In that case, making money is not your primary motivation, and you are best to have these other desires you are trying to fulfill through trading met elsewhere, because other traders will eventually take advantage of your weaknesses.

The most important thing in golf is to keep your eye on the ball while you are in the act of hitting it, and the most important thing for an investor to do is to keep his eyes off of the meaningless market fluctuations and hold firmly and patiently to his positions. One does not try to get rich in one day.

That's not how I thought when I first started out in the stock market. I was obsessed with short-term trading and trying to make huge returns literally overnight. As time has gone by, though, and I have had more and more experience in the stock market, the time frames that I have focused on have been longer in duration, because I have come to real-ize that is where the real money is made. Ironically, it is also much easier to analyze the longer-term trends, which are not prone to noise and meaningless news like the day-to-day trends are, and to invest with them, rather than daytrade or do short-term swing trades that just last a few days.

It is indeed the big trend that is the most important trend. There have been times when I have managed to put all of my money into a sector just starting a brand new bull market. Every year it seems like a new one starts some-where. But the more money I invest into such a position, the harder I have found to hold it for the duration of the bull move. This has been my own weakness.

Only you know what would work best for you, but I believe that the best thing to do is to try not to put all of your money into a stock market trend and try to hold it for the long haul, but instead to hold a core position and trade a portion of the rest of your money accordingly. For example, if you see that oil stocks are about to finish a stage one sideways basing phase and begin a bull market, you may decide to put 20% of your money into a basket of oil stocks and plan to hold them until you believe that the oil stock bull market is over, and then keep the rest of your money aside for another big 20% position in another sector or market elsewhere in the world or for more short-term trading. Or maybe you would prefer to put it in whole other asset classes, like bonds, commodities, or even currencies for diversification—all of which must be analyzed using the same big-picture tools we have talked about together.

The wonderful thing about a bull market is that it doesn't take a huge position to make a lot of money. Twenty percent of your money invested in a core position that doubles in value over a year is a 20% gain for your whole account. Those are the types of years mutual fund managers dream about, but simple money management and some good timing can make them possible for you year in and year out. It all has to do with using a small enough core position that you can hold through a few 10% or 15% corrections without sweating it in order to fully take advantage of the long-term bull trend.

CHAPTER 13:
PROFIT DURING BEAR MARKETS WITH SHORT SELLING

The most profitable way to make money investing is by going long in a group of stocks that belong to a sector of the stock market that is about to begin a bull market and then to hold them until the bull market is over. But money can be made betting against stocks, too. In fact, sometimes in a bear market, that is the only way to make money.

You can bet against an individual stock by doing what is called short selling. When you short sell a stock, you borrow shares for the stock from your broker and then sell them. You have to eventually return these shares. You do that by buying the stock back—called buying to cover—and then returning the shares to your broker.

For instance, if you shorted, say, IBM at $100 a share, you would do that by putting in a short sale order with your broker. After receiving your order, your broker would find some shares available that you could borrow and then sell. The proceeds would then go into your account, and then, when you bought to cover your position and close it out, you would take the price you sold the stock at and subtract the price you bought it for to determine how much money you made or lost on the trade.

So, instead of normally buying a stock and then selling it later, this enables you to sell a stock first and then buy it back at what will hopefully be a lower price. Short sale trades have been going on ever since the first stock exchange opened up hundreds of years ago, so they are nothing new to the stock market, even if they may be new to you.

Most people are scared of the idea of shorting stocks, because in theory if you short something and you hold your short position while the stock goes up to infinity, you could go broke. But just as when you go long, with shorting all you need to do is define how much money you are willing to risk on your trade and put in a stop order—this time a buy to cover stop order—to limit any losses that could occur.

Another reason some people do not like to short stocks is that they are turned off by the idea. They like to go long stocks and root for them and the companies that they represent, so they somehow feel that it is wrong to bet against stocks. However, market makers and floor traders short stocks all of the time in order to maintain order flow. People who buy put options may bet against stocks, too. Shorting is just one tool you can use to make money on the stock market or manage your portfolio.

In fact, the first hedge funds were called hedge funds because people running them would put half of the money into short positions and the rest of it into long positions. That is why they were called hedge funds. Almost no hedge funds do that anymore, and a lot of them use leverage to pyramid themselves up to take bigger risks.

Shorting can be a useful weapon in your arsenal and, at the very least, you need to know how it works. It does take a bit of a different mentality to short stocks then it does to just go long. There are trading strategies on the long side that can work at times which don't translate well to short selling.

For example, in a powerful bull market, you can make money a lot of times by just buying stocks that break out to new fifty-two-week highs, but it is very difficult to make money just by shorting a stock or market index once it makes a new fifty-two-week low. The best and I believe the only effective way to short stocks is to do so by shorting them on a countertrend rally within a stage four bear market downtrend, because stocks in stage four declines are prone to sharp and short-lived countertrend rallies after extended declines that fool the bulls and shake out shorts.

That's a tough thing for most people to do, because in bear markets the financial media tend to get very bullish during bear market rallies, as most people think they represent the beginning of a bull market. As a result, short selling can be a lonely game. At times the media may even blame short sellers for causing market drops, so it is an activity that isn't even worth telling your friends about, especially if you engage in it during a bear market, because they will likely believe what the media tell them to believe and refuse to listen to you or even be resentful of your success.

To make money through short selling means having to completely separate yourself from the crowd and become a pure contrarian, which is something people have a very hard time doing, because if the market goes up they will lose money while others make money. That is just too much for the typical investor to chance. Most investors would rather lose money riding out their long positions with everyone else than try do something that would cause them to lose money while everyone else makes money if it doesn't work.

Those that do get interested in short selling tend to do so towards the end of a bear market and not in the beginning or middle of one when it is most profitable. I know this from my experience from the last two bear markets. In both bear markets, I advocated and presented all sorts of short selling ideas to my premium members, but almost all of them ignored them until we got to the end of the bear market. It was only then that I got lots of e-mails from people who were now shorting stocks in various ways.

The common mistake most of these people would make is to short after the market or a stock fell a lot over the course of several days, instead of shorting after a rally took place. What happens in bear markets is that stocks drop quickly and then have very fast and sharp temporary rallies. But these rallies tend to fool people into thinking that the bear market might be over, so they are too scared to try to short them.

Then, when the rally peaks out and the market drops, people try to short, but do so in a very risky spot, because the more the market falls in a bear market, the more likely it is to have a sharp bounce. If you short after the market drops and then see the Dow rally three hundred points in a day, it is very difficult to not get terrified and cover your position. The only way to prevent this is to wait for a rally to occur and then take some short positions.

This is so hard for the typical investor to do that in a bear market, the average person is probably better off just staying in as much cash as possible and then waiting until the long-term trend changes instead of trying to short. They certainly should not try to trade the market on the long side either, because in a bear market, that is even more difficult than shorting, even though it is what 99% of the people trading the market try to do. More money is lost trying to go long in a bear market than any other way in the stock market.

You may want to allocate a portion of your portfolio to short positions even in bull markets. There is always a sector or individual stock that, for whatever reason, is in a bear market of its own no matter what the conditions of the broad market are. If you are adept at shorting, you may want to always be hedged a certain portion of your portfolio, just in case a new bear market starts or as a way to profit during temporary market corrections.

Back in the 2000-2002 bear market, I made most of my money by shorting individual stocks. The market was in such a sharp down trend that I would short after the market rallied for a few days, then cover a week or so later for profits and then just wait for the next rally to short. I'd use several technical indicators to look for overbought signals to let me know when a good time to short was.

Some things have changed in the investment world over the past decade. Exchange traded funds, which are designed to track an index or sector, proliferated and became popular vehicles for trading the market. These funds trade just like a stock on the stock exchange, so they are easy to get in and out of and provide a lot of liquidity. Some of these funds are designed to go down when the index they are tracking does, and a few are designed to move two or three times the amount the index moves, too.

As a result, in the last bear market, instead of shorting individual stocks, I used these exchange traded funds to make bets against the market for great success. If you want to bet against the market itself, it is much easier to use them than it is to short individual stocks, because with stocks you have to worry about what news can come out on them, and with shorting you must have a more short-term time frame than you do when you normally invest in the stock market, because the stock market over the long-term will go up.

Now sometimes you can short an individual stock that goes to zero. If the stock completely disappeared and ceased to exist, you would simply call up your broker to close out the position. I once shorted a stock that ended up getting halted by the SEC. I got in around $14 a share and covered my position for pennies.

There is a good lesson in this stock, because it can also give you an idea of the perils that can come if you decide to short individual stocks and really become outspoken about it. The symbol of this stock that got halted was GENI—Genesintermedia, Inc. It was run by a few people with extremely shady backgrounds in gun running.

The biggest shareholder in the company was a Saudi Arabian billionaire named Adnan Khashoggi, who was wanted by Interpol for bank fraud. He had been a huge player in the

Iran- Contra arms scandal, reportedly acting as an intermediately in the arms trade. He also worked for Colonel Ghaddafi of Libya. Before the U.S. invasion of Iraq, he met with neoconservative political operative Richard Perle. Khashoggi has been linked to many of the most unsavory events of the past thirty years.

The company had a horrible balance sheet and was bleeding so much cash that it looked like it would eventually go bankrupt. That didn't prevent a CNBC guest from pounding the table on the stock and hyping it to the moon to their viewers, or from sending hundreds of thousands of faxes to people telling them to buy it.

The most interesting thing to me was that Khashoggi not only was the biggest shareholder in GENI but was the biggest short seller in the stock, too! Using offshore accounts, he had shorted enough shares of the stock to completely hedge his long position. This meant that the biggest shareholder in the company had positioned himself to protect his entire investment in the stock, even if it went to zero and had put a complete cap on his upside gains.

Someone involved in the stock even set up a boiler room in Florida to call potential investors and tell them to buy it. I came out as public critic of the stock and shorted it. As a result, I got anonymous e-mails threatening me and telling me to stop talking about it. That just made me want to talk about it even more.

I had shorted the stock at $14 a share, and then one day the stock gapped up to $50 a share thanks to a press release that the company put out claiming to have a financial agreement in place that would supply it with enough money to stay solvent. Of course the deal never happened, and the company eventually went bankrupt.

After the 9/11 terrorist attacks, the Securities and Exchange Commission halted the stock. The U.S. government froze Khashoggi's U.S.-based checking accounts, and he became unable to meet a margin call from the broker that he had shorted the shares with. That broker ended up going bankrupt in what became the biggest payout in the Security Investor Protection Corporation's history.

The point of this is if you want to really get serious about stocks and then short them to make the most money, you need to go after companies that are run by very shady and sometimes dangerous people. You have to ask yourself: is that a game worth playing? It is much easier nowadays to just make money in a bear market using a short exchange traded fund than trying to engage in such battles in individual stocks. If you go public shorting even the biggest and most mainstream of companies, you can still become a target of hatred from the masses of shareholders who populate Yahoo! message boards. All it takes is one nut to cause you grief.

No one hates someone who goes long on a stock trying to make money. But people don't feel the same way about people who bet against stocks, even though that is just as legitimate a thing to do as going long. In fact, short sellers actually provide a lot of benefits to those that play only on the long side of the market.

Short sellers help make the stock market trade more orderly by shrinking the volatility of the market. Remember, short sellers have to buy shares off of the stock exchange in order to close out their positions. The smart short sellers also take advantage of drops in the market to book their profits.

This means that during market corrections, short sellers provide an important source of buying pressure in the market that would not be there otherwise. One of the things that contributed to the fall 2008 stock market crash was the fact that the Securities and Exchange Commission placed a temporary ban on the short selling of bank stocks. As a result, when the market fell that October, there were not a lot of short sellers there to buy these stocks in order to close out their positions.

That made those stocks fall so much that the whole stock market crashed. So when you see the stock market fall hard on any given day, remember the drop really isn't being caused by short sellers, because the smart short sellers don't short on those days but into rallies that happened before them. In fact, the short sellers are helping provide a cushion during market declines. So the market would in fact be falling even faster if they weren't there.

Short selling is a legitimate market activity that the average investor is usually scared of. He often mistakenly thinks that it does him harm, but short selling has no real impact on the long-term trend of the stock market or the economy. There have been times when I have seen companies come out and publicly attack short sellers and blame them for drops in their stocks, but whenever I have seen a CEO do this, he has always been trying to turn attention away from serious problems inside of his company, often of his own creation. Short selling is a useful trading tool that I use occasionally in the stock market and have had spectacular results with during bear markets.

CHAPTER 14:
INVEST IN QUALITY COMPANIES

Most investors claim that they are using fundamental analysis to pick out stocks, but I believe very few actually do this. They say they are buying into growth stocks and usually do it because they hear that the stock has beaten analyst estimates or has been written about in a magazine as a big growth company.

The simple movement of stock prices has more influence over investors than anything else. Some like to buy stocks that fall, thinking they can get a bargain, while others like to chase stocks higher. Whatever the case, most simply buy in reaction to the movement of stock prices and then believe in some story about earnings growth to justify their purchase. They do very little real analysis.

However, most mutual fund managers do pay a lot of attention to earnings estimates and news releases. Mutual funds stay invested in the market all of the time, and the men running them try to beat each other by outguessing each other on which stocks can post the best earnings surprises. They'll try to allocate a portion of their money each quarter to this sort of guessing game.

To me, though, even that isn't using fundamental analysis seriously. Warren Buffett does not decide whether or not to buy or sell a stock based on beating earnings estimates. His sole concern is valuation—whether or not the stock at its current price is truly cheap or not.

That means valuing the true worth of the company and comparing it to the market cap of the stock. Most people who say they use fundamental analysis don't do this, but instead obsess over earnings estimates. That is just about all that is talked about in the financial media, where there is almost never any discussion of the big, meaningful trends of the stock market much less valuation when making an investment decision. The focus is only on earnings growth and hype.

One problem with only looking at earnings growth estimates for companies is that they are based on the projections of Wall Street analysts that tend to be too negative at the bottom of a bear market and the end of a recession and two rosy towards the end a bull market. So you have to be extra careful if you are near the end of a bull market when it comes to growth stocks. Time and time again, once a bear markets begins and the economy starts to slow down, companies fail to meet optimistic analyst projections and have to guide down their expectations.

This can really hurt growth stocks, because they get valuation premiums for being growth stocks. The higher that premium gets—the higher the forward P/E and PEG ratios are—the harder a growth stock can get hit if it fails to meet analyst projections. In the end this isn't something you should get worked up over if you keep a close eye on the overall trend of a stock and use proper stop loss orders to protect yourself if a stock gets hit by bad news or the stock market enters a bear market.

What is more, companies have been known to play accounting games to create earnings growth. But there are some red flags you can watch for in order to know if this might be happening. The simplest is looking at the sales figures for a company. If earnings are growing, but sales are flat or even falling, then the company is probably boosting earnings through temporary measures such as cost cutting, the acquisition of a competitor, and accounting changes. This type of thing can lead to problems later with the growth story of a company.

It is best to buy growth companies that display a pattern of consistent sales growth. Ideally you want to see several years of consistent earnings growth of 25%. You don't want to see growth of 10% one year, then 25%, and then back down to 5% the following year. That means the growth may not be sustainable. If the company has been around for some time, then it is best to see five years of earnings growth of at least 25% a year, and the higher that number, the better.

If you are doing short-term trading with a time frame of holding for several weeks or less, then you don't need to worry about these things too much. But if you are investing in stocks to hold for the long-term, then it is best to make sure you are only buying quality companies. Some other metrics you can look at it to make sure this is the case are the return on equity ratio and the current ratio.

The return on equity ratio is calculated by dividing the net income after tax the company generates by shareholder equity, which is the ownership shareholders have in assets. There can be a negative equity if the company has more liabilities than assets. The return on equity tells you how well a company uses it investment funds to create earnings growth. It gives you an idea of how well the company reinvests its earnings. The best companies have a return on equity over 20%.

On the flip side, you don't want to invest in companies with huge debt loads that might send them into bankruptcy. You can use the current ratio, which divides the current assets by liabilities, to make sure you are investing in companies with solid balance sheets. Companies that have twice as many assets as short-term debt tend to make the best investments, but this ratio is normally bigger with real estate and financial firms.

Most stocks do not pay dividends, because they pile all of their money back into the company in order to create more earnings. But larger and more established companies often pay dividends. Some sectors, such as real estate investment trusts and utilities, pay out high dividends. You can calculate the dividend yield of a stock by dividing the most recent full-year dividend by the current stock price. So, for instance, if a company paid out $1 worth of dividends in the past year and is trading at $20 a share, it has a dividend yield of 5%.

It is well worth having some dividend stocks in your portfolio, because the dividends compound over time, but you cannot just invest solely for dividends when it comes to the stock market. In the end, everything I have told you about picking stocks is more important than buying a stock just because it has a high dividend. In fact, you usually only see huge dividend yields when a stock has declined in price due to perceptions that earnings are going to decline or the company is in trouble. The company will then probably have to cut or even eliminate its dividend.

When looking for short-term trading ideas, I often do not look at these fundamental factors, but when it comes to investing a portion of your money in core positions, you need to stick with quality companies. It is then that these valuation metrics become critical.

CHAPTER 15:
PUTTING IT ALL TOGETHER

This book has been about the timeless principles that are used to make fortunes in the stock market. In it I have given you some specific techniques and chart patterns that I use in my own investing and trading. In fact, I usually look through over two thousand individual stocks every single week in order to find stocks that match both the technical and fundamental criteria I have shared with you in this book.

You can go to my Web site, WallStreetWindow.com, and subscribe to my free e-mail list and find out what I think about the stock market right now. If you are really serious about making money in the stock market, though, I suggest that you take a risk-free trial to my premium service. We even have a special offer for you, because you bought this book. You can find it at WallStreetWindow.com/specialoffer. htm.

I also have a list of other resources you may want to pursue on my Web site, including other books I can recommend that you read if you want to learn more about trading. You can find this by just going to the site and navigating to the resources section. There you will find a list of books that have influenced me the most in my own journey as a trader and some more standard investment reference books.

If you walk into any bookstore, you'll find a bunch of works that will show you in encyclopedic fashion various technical indicators that you can use to interpret the stock market, books on fundamental analysis, and books about the investment fashions of the year. People buy these books and have trouble putting what they read into action and making money, because they don't invest using core principles. They then buy another one, sign up for some stock picks service, or get into black box trading that they hope will just print them money without any effort on their own. They then get disappointed all over again and buy something else. The average person fails to use a real investment strategy and ends up scared and nervous in the market all of the time.

I know how it is, because when I started investing, I read lots of great books and thought I had a strategy that could make money, but I didn't follow through until I got to the point where I had to. All of the stock tips and techniques you might use in the market won't help you without having a solid foundation to work off of. You need to understand what really moves stock prices and how mass psychology is a factor before you can understand your own behavior as an investor.

Then you'll understand that what you need to do is separate yourself from the crowd, focus on the big trend of the market, and enter investments that are aligned with that trend while you take appropriate steps to size up your risks and control them. If you do this, you'll start to invest in the market with confidence. My goal in writing this book is to put you on this path.

It isn't the stock market or stock picks that make you money, but your own ability and foresight as an investor that does. Once you build up those abilities, then you no longer will interact with the stock market in a nervous fashion like everyone else, but instead will approach trading with confidence. It is solid investment principles that never change that create strategic stock trading. Yes, one individual trade may not go right, and you may even get into a trading funk from time to time, but over the long haul, using the right principles is the closest thing to a sure thing you can get out of the stock market.

And that is all about you. It's not about getting lucky. It's about taking responsibility for your money and your results, something the masses refuse to do. I hope to see you as a member of WallStreetWindow and look forward to the years of trading in the stock market that are to come. Remember, who dares, wins!

ACKNOWLEDGEMENTS

Stock charts used in this book provided courtesy of Stock-charts.com.

A NOTE ON THE AUTHOR

Michael Swanson Is the founder and head editor of WallStreetWindow.com. He ran a hedge fund from 2003 to 2006 that generated a return of over 78% for its investors during that time frame and in one year was ranked in the top thirty-five hedge funds among several thousand tracked by hedge-fund.net. Since retiring from the hedge fund industry, he has devoted his time to writing about the financial markets and various other interests. In 2010 he published a book on the history of the American South titled *Danville Virginia, and the Coming of the Modern South*. You can access his views on global market trends by going to WallStreetWindow.com.

Made in the USA
Lexington, KY
28 December 2010